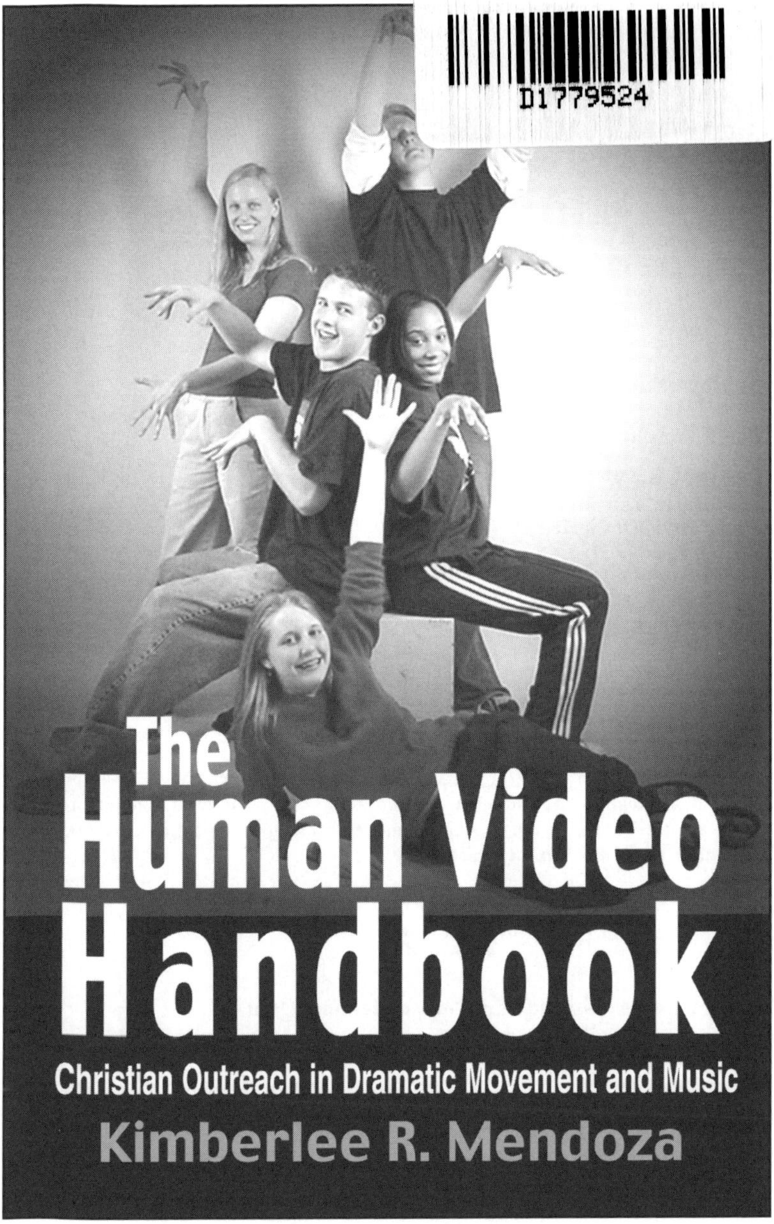

The Human Video Handbook

Christian Outreach in Dramatic Movement and Music

Kimberlee R. Mendoza

MERIWETHER PUBLISHING LTD.
Colorado Springs, Colorado

Meriwether Publishing Ltd., Publisher
PO Box 7710
Colorado Springs, CO 80933-7710

Editor: Rhonda Wray
Cover design: Jan Melvin
Photography: Kimberlee R. Mendoza

© Copyright MMVII Meriwether Publishing Ltd.
Printed in the United States of America
First Edition

All rights reserved. No part of this publication may be reproduced, stored in a retrieval system, or transmitted in any form or by any means, electronic, mechanical, photocopying, recording or otherwise, without permission of the publishers.

Permission to reproduce copies of the worksheet in Appendix A on pages 90-91 and Appendix B on page 92 is granted with the purchase of this book. Copies of these materials are for the use of the purchaser and purchasing organization only and may not be sold or transferred to any third party.

All Scripture is taken from the Contemporary English Version Copyright © 1995 by American Bible Society. Used by permission.

Library of Congress Cataloging-in-Publication Data

Mendoza, Kimberlee R.
  The human video handbook : Christian outreach in dramatic movement and music / by Kimberlee R. Mendoza
    p. cm.
  ISBN-13: 978-1-56608-139-9 (pbk.)
  ISBN-10: 1-56608-139-4 (pbk.)
  1. Pageants. 2. Drama in public worship. 3. Music in churches. I. Title.
PN3203.M46 2007
246'.7—dc22
                        2007021564

To Kelly and Mary Kay

Thank you for your support and encouragement.

I'd be half the artist without you!

Table of Contents

Acknowledgments 1
Introduction 2

Chapter 1
Human Video Defined 3
    What Is a Human Video? 4
    The History of Human Video 4
    What Human Video Is *Not* 5
    The Heart of Human Video 6

Chapter 2
Theatre Basics Applied to Human Video 7
    Understanding the Stage 8
    Acting and Directing 11
    Glossary of Theatre and Human Video Terms 21

Chapter 3
Creating a Human Video *with* Lyrics 23
    Step 1: Determine Your Project 24
    Step 2: Choose Your Song 25
    Step 3: Write Your Script 31
    Sample Human Video Script (with Lyrics) 40

Chapter 4
Creating a Human Video *without* Lyrics 46
    Step 1: Determine the Story 47
    Step 2: Write the Script 49
    Step 3: Choose (or Create) Your Music 54
    Step 4: Workshop the Video 54
    Step 5: Revise the Script 54
    Step 6: List the Props, Costumes, Set, Etc. 55
    Step 7: Draw the Stage Directions 55
    Step 8: Practice Makes Perfect 55
    Step 9: Prepare to Perform 56
    Step 10: Present the Piece 56
    Sample Project 57
    Sample Wordless Human Video Script 60

Chapter 5
Directing a Human Video 63
    Directing Human Video in General 64
    Training a Specific Project — Do's and Don't's 66
    Perfecting the Finished Video 69

Chapter 6
Preparing and Performing a Human Video 75
    Purchase Extra Tracks 76
    Discuss Sound Needs 76
    Obtain the Costumes 76
    Purchase the Props 77
    Practice the Entrances and Exits 77
    Determine the Lighting 78
    Block the Stage 78
    Set Up or Explain the Message 79
    Prepare Spiritually and Physically 79
    Discuss, Evaluate, and Record 80

Chapter 7
Publishing a Human Video 81
    Create the Workbook 82
    Prepare the Packet 85
    Send the Project 86

Appendices 89
    A. Creating Your Wordless Video Worksheet 90
    B. Character Descriptions for the Actor 92
    C. Human Video Song Suggestion List 93
    D. Suggestions for Expressing Emotion
       through Body Language 97
    E. Human Video Resources 100

About the Author 101

Acknowledgments

This book wouldn't be complete if it weren't for the many exceptional people who have supported my journey. I must first acknowledge the editing gifts of my two friends, Mary Kay Moody and Leslie Whaling. You both amaze me.

I also need to express my genuine gratitude to the Faith Evangelism Drama Squad (formerly known as EMT). They are an amazing group of young people who take time from their busy teenage lives to minister through human video in their community. Special thanks to Kelly Krueger, Carolyn Parfet, Thomas Atkins, Maria Palomo, Trisha Mork, Zach Stewart, Andrew Stutz, and Hannah Stutz for modeling for the illustrations in this book. You are such a blessing.

Sean Lambert at Youth With A Mission, San Diego/Baja, thank you for loaning me a minute of your hectic schedule. Also, I'd like to acknowledge David Willsey, Steve Babbitt, Scott Parks, Tony Orlando, Bruce Grecco, John Alexander, Fred Passmore, James Shriver, and Alfred Fragosa for your support.

Jesse Dupuy, I truly appreciate your lending of your artistic talents. I know God is really going to use your amazing ability.

David Dowlen, thank you for allowing me to use your amazing lyrics. May God continue to bless your ministry.

I am grateful to the Faith Chapel staff for the use of the church property and for pouring encouragement into my life daily.

I am blessed to be a part of the San Diego Christian Writer's Guild and am grateful to both the online group and the Spring Valley group for their fabulous ideas and critiques.

To my extended family, your encouragement and support are without measure. I love you very much. I am indebted to my husband, Richard Mendoza, for creating the sound for *The Runner*, and for his constant support of my life. You are a major reason why this book exists. Ricky and Ethan, thank you for giving Mommy an hour here and there to write.

Last, but really first, I thank my Savior, Jesus Christ, for allowing me to serve. Thank you for using me despite my faults.

Introduction

People began acting on the stage long before Christ walked the earth. Greek philosophers used theatre to illustrate their points about religion, Europeans used it as a way of expressing their political views in the form of entertainment, and twentieth-century Americans created plays both for entertainment and as a springboard for political assertions.

Playwrights for millenniums have understood drama to be a powerful tool that speaks to the hearts of an audience. The church, however, saw it as a pagan form of entertainment and shunned the theatre for centuries. In the early seventies, thanks in part to the Jesus Movement, attitudes began to change. Playwrights increasingly turned to religious themes and created such plays as *Godspell* and *Jesus Christ Superstar*. This in turn opened a door for drama in the church. In the 1980s, Christians began to embrace theatre as a useful adjunct to worship and to highlight a minister's message. Through this acceptance, a new form of drama sprang forth — the human video.

This book is intended as a basic guide for anyone who desires to create a poignant ministry through the use of drama and music. It will take you through all the necessary steps:

1. Choosing a song for human video
2. Writing a human video script
3. Directing a human video
4. Preparing a human video
5. Performing a human video
6. Publishing a human video

I've created and taught human video for over fifteen years and would like to share what I've learned along the way. The information in this book will help you perform for youth groups, outreach services, worship services in your own congregation, recovery ministries, street ministry, and more. It will take your drama group to a new level as you share God's message through this awesome new form of drama.

Chapter 1
Human Video Defined

"Music is the only thing that your brain cannot filter. That is why you can be driving, talking on the phone, and eating, and when you get out of the car, you are singing the last song you heard on the radio. Take the power of music and add a compelling illustration of Jesus, and walls that were once up have now come down. Human video opens up doors to people's hearts that no sermon can."

— Scott Parks, Youth Pastor,
Lake Ellsinore First Assembly of God

What Is a Human Video?

Human video is a new type of theatre that combines music, choreography, and drama. Unlike mime, the characters make lifelike movements and don't typically wear traditional clown makeup. The point behind a human video is to portray a strong Christian message using multiple senses. Music is potent. Drama is powerful. Combining the visual art of theatre and the auditory art of music with the message of Jesus Christ is dynamic ministry that speaks to the soul.

In a human video, a song is played while actors use motions to portray a message to the audience. Their movements emphasize both the story and the theme of the song being played.

Human video is ideal for performing in outdoor evangelistic settings, on the mission field, or with a traveling theatre group for two reasons:

1. There is often a minimal set or none at all, and
2. The music is most likely played through a sound system.

These conditions enable a team to come in and perform their piece with little preparation and without worrying if the audience can hear the actors. The wordless human video (discussed in Chapter 6) also transcends language barriers without the need for translation. The motions in a song cross cultures, bringing the salvation message to those of all nationalities.

The History of Human Video

The term "human video" came out of the late 1980s from the concept of the music videos found on such stations as MTV and VH1. The difference between a televised music video and a human video is that a human video is performed live and has a spiritual message.

It is no secret that in the last century the world has been bombarded with visual images from TV, the Internet, billboards, etc. Actors have been performing mime for centuries, but with the creation of the music videos and a visual culture, human video has risen on the scene. In the early years, people called it "mime to music" or "dramatic musical pieces." These performances were first dubbed "human video" at the Pentecostal Fine Arts Festivals, but the name and concept quickly spread into many different Protestant denominations. Several evangelism training schools and missions organizations have embraced the human video because it has the ability to transcend various settings and cultures with its universally understood message.

What Human Video Is *Not*

There are many misconceptions about this medium of theatre. Though human video embraces many of the arts, they do not define it, and its purpose differs as well. Here is a list of things that human video is not:

1. Human Video Is Not Mime

The movements in human video are realistic. The actions aren't exaggerated in a surreal way typical of mime. The characters aren't stuck in a box or leaning on air. Because some ministries do mime to music, one might consider that to be human video, but true human video isn't mime. The actors move in real time, like real people. The motions performed differentiate the two arts.

Additionally, the actors don't usually wear whiteface makeup or black-and-white mime costumes. They often wear matching shirts or costumes that fit the role they are portraying. On occasion, a solo actor may wear the white makeup, but since human video isn't mime to music, it isn't necessary.

2. Human Video Is Not Dance

Though human video involves choreography, it isn't a dance. It is a story set to music, where the characters *act out* the message of a song. Human video is more about the illustration of a song's message than about the actual choreography.

3. It Isn't Interpretive Dance, Either

Although interpretive dance is similar in that it has a message and/or story, human video differs in that its main purpose is to glorify God.

4. Human Video Is Not Entertainment (Alone)

Its primary purpose is to minister, not to entertain. Musical dramas without a message are simply sketches with a song accompaniment and do not qualify as a human video. Though human videos are often entertaining, that isn't their value.

5. Human Video Is Not a Play

Human video characters don't talk. Though there are similarities between plays and human video, a play involves dialog whereas the story of human video comes through the lyrics in the music.

6. Human Video Is Not the Same As a Music Video

A human video is performed live. Many times when people hear the expression "human video," they assume it is the same thing as a music video. The word "human" indicates the difference.

Though human video includes elements of all the above, it is its own art form.

The Heart of Human Video

> "... I do everything I can to win everyone I possibly can"
> (1 Corinthians 9:22).

Human video is about movement and conveying a message. Its main function is to minister to hearts and to beg an emotional response from the audience.

A tremendous bonus about human video is a person doesn't have to be a great actor to perform in one; he or she just needs to have the right heart. A person with a quiet voice or someone who has difficulty speaking or memorizing lines can often do well in a human video. The true artist of human video is the Holy Spirit and his anointing.

Chapter 2
Theatre Basics Applied to Human Video

"The power of human video is that it's done live with real people. Drama is a fantastic tool for creatively touching people's hearts."

— Sean Lambert, President and CEO, Youth With A Mission, San Diego/Baja, and author of the human video *The Redeemer*.

The Human Video Handbook

For those new to drama, we'll look at some basics in the world of theatre:
1. Understanding the stage
2. Tips for acting and directing
3. Terms for theatre and human video

Understanding the Stage

One important thing to remember is the stage is always referred to from the viewpoint of the actor and other performers. Stage Right would be the director's left.

 *A good technique when directing is to cross your arms. If you want the actor to go to the left, you tap your left finger against your right arm and you know it is his or her right, or Stage Right.*

Here is a diagram of a typical stage:

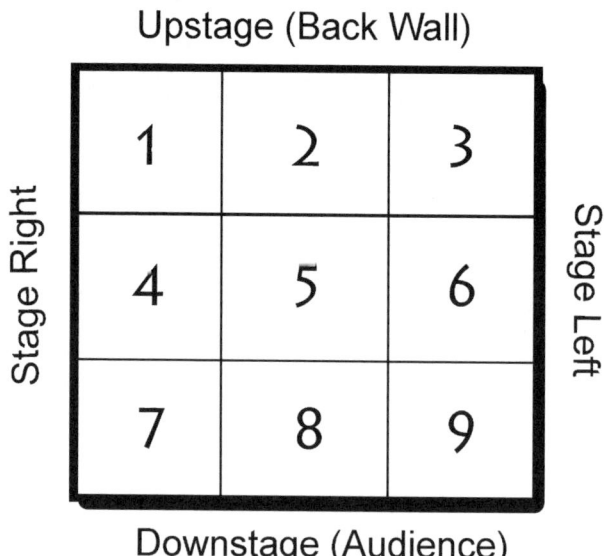

1. Upstage Right
2. Upstage Center
3. Upstage Left
4. Center Right
5. Center Stage
6. Center Left
7. Downstage Right
8. Downstage Center
9. Downstage Left

Writing Stage Directions

When writing a normal stage play, there is little direction and a lot of dialog. When writing a film script, there is plenty of both direction and dialog. When writing a human video, there is only direction. The dialog comes from the lyrics in the song, so the director and actors have to visualize the story through the stage directions.

Different Types of Stage Directions:
Physical Action — *(JOHN sat down.)*
Implicating Action — *(JOHN paused.)*
Emotional Action — *(JOHN is upset.)*
Clarifying Action — *(JOHN turned to MARY.)*

Stage Positions

When considering stage positions, take into account the audience's view of the actor and the relation of each actor to each of the other actors.

1. *Full Front* — Completely facing audience.
2. *One-Quarter* — Slight angle to audience.
3. *Profile* — Side view of character.
4. *Three-Quarter* — Angled away from audience.
5. *Full Back* — Completely turned from audience.

6. Shared
Both actors stand facing each other.

7. Upstaging
One actor steps in front of another actor.

8. Zero Position
Standing at attention, with hands at one's sides and feet together.

The various stage positions tell the audience different things. *Full front* is a position of strength, while *three-quarters* is a sign of weakness. In human video, *full back* is considered off-stage. Instead of leaving the stage, an actor turns his or her back to indicate being out of the current action. *Shared* shows relationship, and often profile conveys conflict. Unless it helps with what you're trying to portray, *upstaging* should be avoided at all cost. *Zero position* is used in human video as a starting and ending point.

Acting and Directing

Acting is the art of becoming someone other than oneself. It involves pretending, emotional recall, and physical movement. Though human video doesn't always demand the best actors, here are some tips that can help your actors portray the message in a more powerful way.

Get in Touch with Your Emotions

Human video involves intense feelings, such as passion, angst, depression, sorrow, or joy. The better an actor can portray these emotions, the stronger his or her performance will be, and the more it will move the audience. The point to theatre is to not appear as if one is acting, but rather truly experiencing a situation. The key — don't *try* to act. Instead, seek to feel what the character is feeling.

(See Appendix D for emotion ideas.)
Emotion:
- Moves the audience
- Drives a scene
- Helps the performance
- Mirrors life

EXERCISE

Ask your actors to write down different personal experiences and how they made the actors feel. Then suggest that they use those feelings in each scene. If someone has never experienced a certain emotion, encourage him or her to try to imagine what it would be like. For instance, let's say there is an actor who needs to mourn the death of a friend, but he's never experienced death. You could suggest imagining how he'd feel if his favorite pet died.

To turn on emotions, try this exercise. Ask the actor to take in a big gulp of air into the back of his or her throat until it clicks, then let it out slowly while thinking about a particular emotion.

Develop the Skill of Sensory Memory

It is important for an actor to get in touch with all five senses: touch, taste, smell, hearing, and sight. Senses determine how we view the world. Sensory memory can also help an actor (and audience) feel an experience more intensely. For example, when an actor pretends to take a bite of an apple, if he or she can recall how crunchy, juicy, and sweet it is in real life, then the audience will likely be convinced by the actor's facial expression.

EXERCISE

Ask each actor to sit facing a partner. Place an object in each one's hand (such as a rabbit's foot, sandpaper, ice cube, etc.). With each new sensation, encourage them to mentally file away the other actor's response. After each actor has experienced a variety of items, progress to putting a flavor on each one's tongue (pickle, chocolate). Follow with holding strong-smelling items under each one's nose (vinegar, vanilla), playing sounds (ocean, grinding metal gears), and showing photos (baby, spider). You could also have them do this in front of a mirror to help them remember how they looked when experiencing a certain sense. They should experience the sensation of the object and then hold their expression as they look in a mirror.

Learn to Imitate Natural Movements

It is especially important in human video that an actor understands how one's body looks and reacts to different things. A sad person might be slumped and brooding. A happy person would likely be open and friendly, while an angry person would be closed, with arms folded and eyes diverted. Unlike in mime, a body in human video needs to move about the stage as it would in day-to-day life. If an actor learns how people like his or her character act, it will hopefully enable that actor to recreate the role more authentically. For instance, if the role calls for someone to play the part of an elderly gentleman, that actor may consider visiting the older adult ministry at his or her church. Watching movies or plays may also help with recreating mannerisms and personality quirks of certain characters.

EXERCISE

Ask your actors to keep daily journals, entering the things and people they see around them. Direct them to sit in a park, at a bus stop, or in the mall to watch people interact with one another and then jot down what they see.

Practice the Art of Relaxing On-stage

Relaxing is important to any good performance. A relaxed actor will appear more realistic, and the audience will feel more at ease. Several things can help an actor to feel less anxious in the presence of people and lights. They need to learn to breathe at a normal pace. Encourage them to take deep breaths, inhaling and exhaling, several times before going on-stage. Also, teach them to focus on a certain spot in the auditorium above the audience or on their fellow actors.

EXERCISE

Before every performance, roll the shoulders and stretch the neck side to side. Breathe in deeply. (See exercises in Chapter 6 for more ideas.)

 *Avoid caffeinated beverages and drink lots of water.*

Learn to Maintain a Make-Believe World

Good human video actors are able to focus all of their attention on their characters and the imaginary environment provided by the lyrics in the song. Some theatre people call this a "bubble." Staying inside this bubble will help the audience enter into the fantasy world and forget the actor is acting. It is best that the actors avoid eye contact with the audience so they will not divert their attention away from the action in the human video. A good way to preserve this is to really work at becoming one's character and tuning out any reality other than the one on-stage.

EXERCISE

Challenge the actors to get to know their characters really well by writing down their attributes (see the Character Development Worksheet in Appendix B). Encourage them to spend a lot of time thinking about how their characters would act in the pretend scene.

Develop the Imagination

The art of acting is the gift of imagination. A good actor can always imagine a certain situation in his or her head. He or she is able to picture him or herself as that person and understand how the person moves, thinks, and feels. The more a person can get in touch with the childhood ability to pretend, the better an actor he or she will be. The fake props and the emotions of a made-up situation will become real to the actor, and thus to the audience.

EXERCISE

Give your actors a magazine picture showing people interacting. Have them pretend to be the people in the setting of the picture, acting out an impromptu scene.

Learn to Localize Body Movements

People forget about their body when they first start acting, but human video is all about the body. It is important for actors (and directors) to know how one's hands, head, shoulders, feet, etc. should be placed for different emotions. For example, if someone were bored, his or her posture would be relaxed. If a person were anxious, he or she might fidget. (See Appendix D, "Suggestions for Expressing Emotion through Body Language," for more suggestions.)

Additionally, if more than one actor is to perform the same movement at the same time, it's crucial that all their limbs take on the same shape and that the action occurs on the same plane. Are the fingers cupped or flat? Are the elbows bent or straight? Are the feet parallel with the shoulders or are they farther out? These are all questions that you will have to answer when directing your human video. (See Chapter 5, "Perfecting the Finished Video," for more ideas.)

EXERCISE

Ask your actors to tell about their day and how it made them feel without moving their hands or head. Then have them do it again, slowly allowing them to move one part of their body at a time to emphasize their words. For instance, "I am so tired." A person who is tired might begin to lower his or her eyes to half-mast. His or her hips might then tilt to the side, and his or her shoulders would probably come down to a slumped posture.

Begin to Develop and Understand a Character

Accomplished actors can identify with their characters in some way. They have empathy for what their characters are going through and are motivated to change the bad and embrace the good. The closer an actor can get to the character's emotion, the more convincing he or she will be in that role.

Prompt the actors to ask themselves the four "Character W's":
- *Who* am I? (Personality)
- *Where* am I? (Location)
- *What* do I want? (Desire)
- *Why* do I care? (Emotion)

EXERCISE

Go to Appendix B and fill out the Character Development Worksheet. This will enable the actor to fully understand his or her character.

Focus on Understanding the Story

An important element to acting is not only understanding the characters in the piece, but also understanding the conflict of the story. In order for an actor to perform realistically in a situation, he or she needs to first comprehend it. This is particularly true in human video. The story's passion comes through the actor's emotions and body language. The more an actor adopts the message, the stronger his or her performance will be.

EXERCISE

Explain the story behind the human video you are working on and ask the actors to not only repeat what you've told them, but also share how it applies to their individual lives.

Give Your Performance to God

The quality that makes drama in the church great isn't the talent or resources found in traditional theatre. As a matter of fact, those things are sometimes lacking. What makes drama in the church amazing is the anointing of the Holy Spirit on the lives of the actors. Therefore, always encourage heart over talent. Find ways to give God the glory. Be sure to invite him to every practice and performance. Keep him as the focus, and never doubt for a moment that he is proud of the performers for their effort. I guarantee God won't be upset with the lack of ability, but rather delighted with the passionate heart of ministry.

EXERCISE

The best thing a group can do is to spend time praying. Put on a worship CD and then lead them in prayer and encourage them to share their needs. This will not only help the actors to bond but will also keep the focus where it belongs.

Ten Acting No-No's

As a director, actors will need some general guidance. Here are ten "no-no's" that actors need to avoid.

1. Don't bend toward the person you're interacting with.
Do maintain natural posture. A lot of new actors tend to bend forward to show the audience whom it is they are addressing, but that isn't a natural stance. In human video, it looks odd and can distract from the message. Actors should avoid cocking the head or leaning forward at the waist when it isn't part of the scene.

2. Don't make eye contact with the audience.
Do stay within your bubble. As already mentioned earlier in this book, the audience needs to feel lost in the created world. If an actor makes eye contact with them, then that bubble is popped. The cast should, as already mentioned, pretend there is a wall between themselves and the audience. Think of it this way: If two people were having a conversation, it would seem odd if someone kept looking at the wall. Since there is a "wall" between the actor and the audience, he or she needs to keep his or her focus on the other actors.

3. Don't let hands go out of character.
Do use hands to emphasize emotions. Actors need to avoid putting their hands in their pockets, playing with their costumes, hanging onto set pieces, or fiddling with props. These movements make them appear nervous and out of character.

They should only draw on gestures that their characters would use. For instance, a businesswoman probably wouldn't be giving a high five, and surfers wouldn't likely drink tea with their pinky fingers sticking out.

4. Don't be afraid of being touched.
Do act naturally. Sometimes in human videos, people need to hug or touch. Many of the human videos that I've directed involve people falling into Jesus' arms. An actor needs to learn to be comfortable with his or her team members and not be afraid of physical contact or touching others if the character needs to. One mistake new actors make is leaning a foot forward to hug or barely embracing another actor. The audience doesn't believe the connection for a second. The hug has to be real to emphasize a shared emotion.

Plan a fun activity to help your team become more comfortable with one another. Arrange for a movie night, bowling, hanging out at the beach, etc. Often the issue isn't the acting as much as the interpersonal chemistry.

5. Don't move without reason.
Do move with purpose. The actors should have a motive to change positions, and they should not move aimlessly about the stage. Random movement makes the audience antsy and the actor look nervous. They should move only when directed to do so.
They should avoid shifting their weight back and forth from one foot to the other or bouncing. Actors should also avoid pacing back and forth on the stage for an extended period of time. This makes the audience dizzy and uncomfortable.

6. Don't be afraid to take advice.
Do glean the knowledge of others. Often both the actors and directors can benefit from the advice of other directors and/or other actors. Even veterans still learn from the expertise of someone else. We can all benefit from the eyes of someone not close to the project. Often someone more removed from the production who just happens to be watching can spot a flaw that the actor or director doesn't.

7. Don't mistake passion for acting in an unnatural way.

Do use authentic actions. Have you ever heard of the expression "over the top"? This is referring to someone who has overplayed his or her part. Passion is an emotion that shows conviction, but acting melodramatically in an unnatural way is a surreal emotion that weakens what is happening.

On the other hand, make sure your actors don't perform like robots. Unless it is an action-driven human video, the acting needs to appear natural. Remember, human video isn't mime. Rather, it is imitating real people with real problems.

8. Don't emphasize mistakes.

Do stay in character at all times. If an actor messes up, goes the wrong way, comes in late, or does the wrong motion, the audience may forgive the mistake (or may not even notice) — unless the actor breaks character. The actors need to stay in character no matter what happens. This starts in practice. If they are encouraged to keep going, even in the beginning stages, they will be more likely to do so on-stage.

9. Don't forget to fully utilize props.

Do be aware of all necessary props, even the fake ones. This is especially true with pantomimed props. Often new actors forget to put down or pick up props.

EXERCISE

Instruct your team to walk through a simple task, such as brushing their teeth. As they mime brushing their teeth, the rest of the team watches and writes down what motions they're forgetting. Did they remember to unscrew the cap off the tube? Did they remember to turn the faucet on and off? Did they set the tube down before brushing their teeth? Every step counts in human video.

10. Don't upstage the other actors.

Do be aware of all the players. Upstaging is walking in front of other actors on-stage (not including the full back position). Blocking is like a puzzle. It is important to space people in such a way that when one moves, so does another person. Actors need to be aware of the other actors at all times so that they don't move in front of them.

Acting Do's and Don't's

DON'T	DO
Don't bend toward the person you're acting with.	**Do** maintain a natural posture.
Don't make eye contact with the audience.	**Do** stay within your bubble.
Don't let hands go out of character.	**Do** use hands to emphasize emotions.
Don't be afraid of being touched.	**Do** act naturally.
Don't move without reason.	**Do** move with purpose.
Don't be afraid to take advice.	**Do** glean the knowledge of others.
Don't act in an unnatural way.	**Do** use authentic actions.
Don't emphasize mistakes.	**Do** stay in character at all times.
Don't forget to fully utilize props.	**Do** be aware of all props.
Don't upstage the other actors.	**Do** be aware of all players.

Chapter 2 — Theatre Basics Applied to Human Video

Glossary of Theatre and Human Video Terms

Here are a few general theatre terms that may help you when writing your script and directing your cast.

About Face	Turning completely around in one motion.
Actor	The person performing.
Apron	The area in front of a closed curtain.
Backstage	Behind the main curtain.
Beat	Half of a pause.
Bit Part	A small role.
Blackout	When all the lights go out at once.
Block	Figuring out where each character will stand for each part of a performance.
Book	The script.
Call	The time cast members are to arrive.
Cheat Out	To angle more toward the audience.
Choreography	Planned movements of people and things.
Claw	To bend fingers toward each other.
Crisp	Sharp movements.
Cross Stage	To move from one position to another.
Cue	A signal to the actor or crew to begin a line or an action.
Cutout	A cardboard piece of scenery.
Director	The person responsible for bringing a script to life.
Dressing Off	Placing one's arm out to another actor to measure distance apart.
Dressing Set	Adding pictures, furniture, props, etc.
Entrance	Where an actor enters the scene.
Flat	A two-dimensional piece of scenery held by a frame.
Fly	To elevate scenery by means of a pulley, ropes, etc.

Gel	A thin sheet of colored plastic used to color the lights.
House	Where the audience sits.
House Lights	Lights that illuminate the auditorium.
Lyrics	Words to a song.
Mask	To conceal a person, prop, or set from the audience.
Mime	To pretend an action or object is real.
Pause	A moment of hesitation in a script.
Prop	A hand-held item.
Rake	A stage floor that slopes.
Scene	A part of a story in a script.
Set	Scenery or a background for a play.
Sight Lines	Line of vision from the extreme positions in the house.
Spike	A marked spot where a prop or person should be placed.
Spotlight	A single light used to highlight a specific actor or prop.
Spirit Fingers	Moving fingers rapidly in the air.
Stage	The area where the performance takes place.
Stage Lights	Lights that illuminate the stage.
Wings	Off-stage areas out of the sight lines.
Zero	Back to starting position.

Chapter 3
Creating a Human Video *with* Lyrics

"Human videos are the greatest dramatic visual which sparks the Spirit to ignite the heart for response."

— Rev. Tony Orlando, Student Ministries Pastor, Faith Chapel

When creating a human video with lyrics, there are many things that will need to be considered. The two main ones are: 1. How big is your group?, and 2. Who is your audience? The next few pages will walk you through the steps of how to prepare a human video.

Step 1: Determine Your Project

Before you can decide on a song, you need to determine what type of human video you'd like to do. Ask yourself these questions:

Who is the audience?
Where is your location?
How big is your team?
What would you like to be the end result?

The answers to these questions will help you decide the kind of video you would like to produce.

Human videos fall into two main categories and four purpose types.

Human Video Categories

Story-Driven

This is a human video created from a song with lyrics that tell a story. For example, a woman is hurting and a man is sick. Jesus heals them. This scenario is *story-driven*.

There are two kinds of story-driven human videos:
- *Line-by-Line*. This is a literal interpretation of what the lyrics say.
- *Free-Moving*. This free-form human video tells a story without following the words verbatim.

Action-Driven

This video has a powerful message without a specific storyline. Though there isn't a story, the message still holds impact. Many times this kind of human video involves military-type movements and is enacted by large groups.

Chapter 3 — Creating a Human Video with *Lyrics*

Human Video Purpose Types
The categories above determine the structure, and the purpose types below determine your motivation.

Solo Human Video
Performed by only one person.

Message-Driven Human Video
A powerful human video with a profound message. This is often used when trying to encourage a congregation or a group of people who are hurting. It revolves around a topic or issue — for example, it may stress the importance of missions or remind us that God is not far away.

Evangelistic Human Video
An emotional human video with a salvation message. This is similar to a message-driven human video, except it has one audience — those who are not believing Christians.

Worshipful Human Video
A human video set to a worship song.

Now that you have an idea of what kind of video you'd like to do, it is time to select a song.

Step 2: Choose Your Song

Recognizing a Good Song
First and foremost, you need to pick the perfect song for your project/message. Without a song, you have a skit — not a human video.

Selecting a song can be tricky. People often approach me with a song that they love and think would make a great human video. What they don't realize is that there is more to picking a song for human video than just liking a sound or the words.

Think of human video as a sermonette (a small sermon). It is either a precursor to the pastor's message or it *is* the message. Therefore, the song must have certain qualities to achieve this goal.

If the chosen musical piece keeps you from your goal, scrap the song and pray that God will give you another one.

A good human video song has the following:

Understandable Lyrics

If the message can't be understood, you've lost the reason for performing the human video. Sometimes we know a song really well, but when the audience hears it, they can't understand the words. It is important that the message isn't lost in the music. For example, I love Christian punk and alternative music. But most good human video songs can be classified as "bubblegum pop" music. Why would a hard-core music listener such as I use such mellow-sounding songs for human video? Because the lyrics are comprehensible to a mass audience.

That's important most of the time. There is one exception. Assume that your audience is a room full of punk rock kids with spiked hair and tattoos. They may not appreciate a Michael W. Smith or Ray Boltz ballad, so a harder rock sound could be appropriate. Keep in mind, however, that sometimes even the heaviest of bands perform a good ballad now and then.

Just remember — whatever you choose, *keep the message first.*

Lyrics That Avoid Ambiguity

Make sure the message of the song's story is clear. Sometimes the music in a song sounds great and the words are clear, but the audience is still lost. This happened to me a few years back. My team was asked to perform for an evening worship service at our church. I found a song that the team and I loved. It had great sound, wonderful movements, and was fun to do — however, the audience's response was lukewarm. Why? Because the story wasn't clear and had to be explained. Since they couldn't understand the story, we lost them. It was too ambiguous.

Also, try to understand your audience. Where do you gauge they are at spiritually, mentally, emotionally, and physically? These factors will influence what song is best.

Lyrics That Make a Point

Message, message, message. The concept behind human video is to strike a chord in someone's heart. The lyrics need to tell a story and/or make a strong point. There needs to be a beginning, a middle, and an end. There must be a spiritual reason for the human video: Is there a solution to the character's problem? Is the message clear? Does the song evoke a response? Does it change someone's life in a clear way?

It isn't always important for the human video to be based on a story, but the message must be apparent. Carman's "America Again" is a great example of how a human video can have a message and not a story. When I direct this song, I have six people act out motions to the lyrics. The song is about the destruction of America brought on by the idea of removing God from our country. It isn't a story, but more like a sermon. The motions just help bring Carman's message out visually for the audience. The lyrics alone have a strong enough message to evoke an emotional reaction, and it is a song that does well both in the church and in evangelistic settings.

Please don't try to cover the whole Bible in one human video. Like a sermon, it needs to address one topic, whether that is forgiveness, mercy, salvation, etc. Think of the parables Jesus told. Sean Lambert, author of the Youth With A Mission human video *The Redeemer*, puts it best: "Jesus used tremendous creativity when he told passionate stories and parables in his day. These parables covered various elements of the gospel and God's nature and character. A human video can act like a modern-day parable, capturing the attention of people and pointing them to a God who loves."

Resolution

It's important that the audience walks away with some sort of hope or understanding about what action they need implemented into their spiritual life. Just like in a good book or movie, a human video must work toward a resolution.

Several years ago, a powerful song about a school shooting made its debut. Everyone on my team thought it was awesome and assumed it would make a great human video. It had a definite story, clear lyrics, and an amazing beat. The problem? The song left the audience hanging because it had no clear resolution. It ended with a bunch of teenagers dead and without any prospect of redemption. I couldn't direct a human video that doesn't show some sort of hope. What would be the point?

I have addressed controversial subjects before, but they always had a positive outcome. For example, in the 1980s, DeGarmo & Key had a song called "Teenage Suicide." In the human video, three people act out the motions of suicide. That in itself could be a pretty dark story, but the song doesn't stop there. At the end of the song, a fourth person comes out and reveals that he too could have been a suicide victim, but Jesus came into his life and saved him. A subject like suicide is tough. The point to performing a song like "Teenage Suicide" is to help those who deal with such issues. But there *must* be hope. A good human video will always leave the audience with an ending that can change a life. Resolution is your final testimony. It's what makes the audience cry or fall to their knees. It's your most important element. Don't create a human video without it.

It Isn't Repetitious

Once you begin putting movement to your lyrics, you'll understand this factor. Most of the time songs with repetitive lyrics make lousy human videos. This is because actors are forced to do the same movements over and over. This is boring for the audience and frustrating for the actor.

When picking a song, make sure the lyrics have several verses. Try to avoid songs that are almost all chorus. Look for songs with a story in the verses. For example, Crystal Lewis's song, "In Return," has three separate verses that address three different issues: feeling broken-hearted, being empty, and poverty. In the human video (created by Jeremy Nicks), the first woman is broken-hearted, the second woman is empty, and the last one is poor. Ms. Lewis sings about one story and then sings the chorus. By hearing a different story dispersed between the choruses, the audience has the opportunity to breathe and the motions look less tedious.

It Fits the Audience

The audience may not appreciate your choice of song for many reasons. The basis for some of these have already been discussed, such as ambiguity, hard-to-understand lyrics, and the beat. But another turnoff could also be the message.

There are songs I will perform at my church that I would never perform in an outreach setting. For instance, a song about helping the homeless is a great song to encourage outreach, but it would be absurd at a rescue center. By the same token, a human video about teenage suicide wouldn't be appropriate in a home for the elderly. Consider who your target audience is and how they will most likely respond to the message.

Knowing Where to Look for Songs

There are several different ways to find songs. Here are just a few that have worked for me.

Purchase a Compilation CD

A good way to know what is out there without buying a bunch of CDs is to purchase a compilation mix of various artists. Usually bands put their best songs on these albums in hopes that you'll purchase their CD. Many of my human videos have come from buying annual sampler CDs, such as *WOW* and *Dove Hits* from the Dove Awards.

Listen to Christian Radio

If you have a local station or can access one on the Internet, flip it on. Many times while driving in my car, I'll hear a song that ministers to me. I figure that if it touches my heart, there is a strong possibility it will minister to someone else, too.

Ask Friends

If you have friends that are (or have been) involved in their church's drama ministry, ask them about any human videos they've been in or seen. Also, ask your friends to be on the look out for a good song. People often give me songs to listen to. (Just make sure they meet the criteria already discussed.)

Contact Drama Groups

E-mail or call other drama leaders to find out some of the human videos that they have performed. You may even try to catch a few performances to glean ideas. If you don't know of any offhand, you can search the Internet or call local churches. You may also consider contacting CITA (Christians in Theatre Arts) at http://www.cita.org.

Consider Your Old Collection

Don't discount old songs. Some of them have incredibly powerful messages. So what if it's on 8-track or vinyl? If you think the song works for human video and has the ability to change lives — use it. I suggest going on the Internet and searching for the album. There's a chance it has been made into a CD. If not, consider asking a band to play it live with a more current sound.

Ask Your Pastor

A lot of times, pastors have a vision of where they plan to go in a sermon series. Talk to your pastor about themes and/or see if there is a song he or she would like to use.

Watch Christian Music Videos on DVD or TV

Occasionally there are music videos on TV or for purchase at Christian bookstores. Music videos are wonderful for inspiring a story and giving great visual clues to creating a human video. You also get a peek at what the artist was thinking when he or she created the lyrics.

Consider Some Secular Songs

Occasionally, there is a secular song that has a powerful salvation message. For example, on my song list (see Appendix C), I've included Billy Joel's "We Didn't Start the Fire." When I listened to the song, I could picture the fall of man and how one act of disobedience destroyed mankind. At the end of the human video, I show that the world is still hurting, but Christ's sacrifice on the cross stops the fire. It is possible to use a secular song if the message is clear.

Search the Internet

Go to a search engine, such as Google or Yahoo, and type in "Christian music lyrics." Usually, several Web sites will come up with all sorts of artists to choose from. Then look through the lyrics for a song that fits your message. You might also consider going to a cyber-space garage sale, such as Amazon or eBay.

Visit a Christian Bookstore

There are several benefits to going to a Christian bookstore. You can speak to a clerk to see if he or she has any recommendations, you can look through songbooks, and/or if the store has the technology, listen to various CDs. This way you can find the right song before you purchase it.

Step 3: Write Your Script

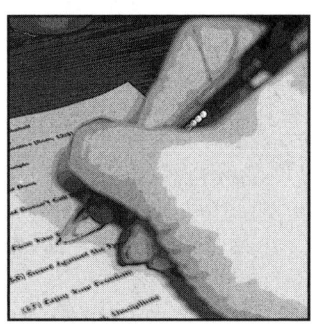

Now that you know what kind of human video you'd like to do and you have a song, it's time to print off those lyrics and get started.

There are many different ways in which people create human videos. Some people listen to a song and start plugging in ideas with the actors present. Some people write a story and then try to find a song to fit. I prefer making a script from a song I've already chosen. This enables me to split my team up to work on several projects. It also gives me something to refer to later if I choose to use the human video again.

Type Out Lyrics and Save Them on Your Computer

Typing out the lyrics on the computer will enable you to make changes to your stage directions later. Always double-space the lyrics to make room for your stage directions. (Note: Be aware of any copyright laws that exist. Some lyrics may be found or purchased on the Internet, while others are in the public domain.)

Here is an example of typing out the lyrics:

Song Title: *"Jesus, My Friend"*

Sunday morning I roll out of bed,

It's God's time today.

Clear my mind and my head

So that I can finally pray.

Chorus:
Jesus, my Savior, my Lord, my friend,

Help me to turn to you once again.

Capitalize and Bold the Main Nouns and Capitalize and Underline the Action Verbs

Nouns and verbs are the words that help you determine your movement.

"Jesus, My Friend"

Sunday morning I <u>ROLL</u> out of **BED**,

It's **GOD'S** time **TODAY**.

<u>CLEAR</u> my **MIND** and my **HEAD**

So that I can finally <u>PRAY</u>.

CHORUS:
JESUS, my **SAVIOR**, my **LORD**, my **FRIEND**,

<u>HELP</u> me to <u>TURN</u> to **YOU** once again.

Determine What the Song Means and What You Want Your Story or Message to Portray

Is your message about a man who needs to find God? Is it about letting go of the world? Is it about helping others? Once you figure out what the true message behind the lyrics is, then you will be able to work toward portraying visually what your heart tells you. For the lyrics "Jesus, My Friend," the message is about living for Jesus every day of the week.

Visualize Your Story

Listen to the song straight through. Visualize who the characters will be, what they will do, and the story that will be told.
- Are the characters logical and realistic?
- Are the characters needed in the drama?
- Do they help the message or do they hinder it?
- Do they have a definite dilemma or meaning behind their actions?

- Can the audience tell what the problem is?
- Is the audience able to identify with what is going on?
- Do the characters face a clear dilemma?
- Do they search for and find meaning in a challenge?
- Do their actions make sense?

Write Out the Motions

Now that you've typed out the lyrics, determined what the song means, and visualized the song's story, you're equipped to start writing the motions to the song.

A few simple style tips will make your instructions easier to be read quickly and be understood. Under each line in the lyrics (remember, you double-spaced), write the motions you visualized as stage directions in upper- and lower-case italics and enclose them in parentheses. The motions are physical movements to the verbs, which give meaning to the nouns. Type the character names in all-capital letters so you can tell at a glance who is doing what.

Write the Chorus Motions First

Your chorus is an essential part of a human video. It is done the most and can be the most powerful element. It is important that the chorus stands out.

Here is an example of some actions applied to a chorus:

CHORUS:
Jesus,
(Arms sweep out to the sides as if you were on a cross.)

My Savior,
(Hands come to middle of chest with palms facing up, and eyes skyward.)

My Lord,
(Clasp hands and inhale deeply enough that the shoulders come forward.)

My friend,
(Bring prayer hands to chin and close eyes.)

Help me to turn to you once again.
(Fall to knees.)

Note on the last line that I didn't have the person follow the verb "turn." It made more sense to have them fall to their knees. Sometimes making them follow the lyrics exactly can make the story seem awkward or trite. Go with what works best for the story.

Write the Verse Motions

Now you're ready to complete the human video by writing the motions to the verses. As already mentioned, I often capitalize the lyrics and sometimes even bold them. If you have a color printer, selecting a different color for the motions might also be helpful. Here's an example of motions to the first verse of "Jesus, My Friend."

"Jesus, My Friend"

Sunday morning I roll out of bed,
(PERSON 1 rolls out of bed, rubbing eyes.)

It's God's time today.
(With left hand, grabs and looks at Bible.)

Clear my mind and my head
(Brings right palm to forehead and then pushes hand away with palm out to audience.)

So that I can finally pray.
(Brings Bible to chest and clasps both hands in front with head bowed.)

Individual Stage Direction Ideas

You're just starting to write a human video. What should you have your actors *do*? When you're new to this art form, you don't always know how to describe the motions you wish to use, or you lack ideas. Here are a few common movements that I use:

All of Me — *(Hands push down over body.)*
Bible — *(Cup hands.)*
Breathe — *(Hand at mouth, fingers closed, push out and open hand.)*
Burden — *(Pick up load and place it on shoulders.)*
Calm — *(Hand spans in front, palm down.)*
Crying — *(Rub eye or cheek.)*
Drinking — *(Make fist and bring to mouth.)*
Drugs — *(Pinch thumb and index finger together and put to lips as if smoking.)*
Go (or Going) — *(Step forward one exaggerated step.)*
Healing — *(Arms sweep up and cross over chest.)*
Heart — *(Grasp chest and pull out with clawed fingers.)*
Holy Spirit Anointing — *(Run spirit fingers over body.)*
Hungry — *(Grab stomach.)*
Jesus (or Cross) — *(Arms out to each side.)*
Lonely — *(Circle hand over face.)*
Love — *(Cross hands over chest.)*
Me — *(Hit chest with hand.)*
Mind — *(Hands turn in circles next to each ear.)*
Money — *(Pinch and rub fingers together.)*
Prayer— *(Clasp fingers and bow head.)*
Shame — *(Run hand in front of face and look down.)*
Strength — *(Flex arm at side.)*
Torn — *(Bring fists together and twist them in opposite directions.)*
Wake — *(Put hands over eyes, tilt head back and flip hands out.)*
Salvation — *(Pull heart from chest, look up and put arm over head.)*

Group Movement Ideas

Action-driven, large group human videos can look amazing! The more movements the actors do together, the better. Here are some powerful movements that look great with bigger groups:

- About-faces and crisp turns
- Tilt to the side or back
- Step forward or sideways in unison
- Lift someone in the air
- Hands in the air
- Fall (knee) to the ground
- Start with heads down and look at the audience at the same time.

Training and Research for More Movements

Some motions in human video are overdone, and as you create your own human videos, it's easy to get in a rut. In the last few years, I have begun to look for ways to inspire new ideas. When I consider different disciplines, I am able to see new avenues for my group to express themselves. For instance, American Sign Language is great for hand motions. Dance is wonderful for the body. Though human video isn't defined by any other art form, it can borrow ideas from them. Here are just a few concepts that you might look into to help you create expressions of movement.

Aerobic Tape/DVD
Though it might be a bit unconventional, some exercise tapes or DVDs have some great movements.

American Sign Language (ASL)
ASL has a lot of motions that may be used to express a certain emotion or object. Consider buying a book or taking a class to learn more.

Charades
In order for a team to win at a game of charades, a person must be able to discern what physical action is being portrayed. This is done through movement.

Cheerleading
Since cheerleading is essentially a group moving in sync to a choreographed routine with crisp motions, there is some potential "borrowing material" here, especially for action-driven human videos involving a large group.

Dance
Though human video isn't dance, it does involve choreography. The use of some dance moves could give a unique flair to your project, especially in action-driven human videos.

There are all sorts of styles to choose from: ballet, interpretive, hip hop, line, swing, etc.

Illusion

Christian illusions are tricks that can often help with the message of a story. If you're interested in ideas, you may go to http://www.christianillusion.net.

My team has performed a few illusions in conjunction with human video. Our greatest one involves Carman's song "The Champion." The song is about the Crucifixion and Jesus' ability to combat hell and the grave and, ultimately, sin. In the human video, Jesus is stabbed by Satan and locked in a box. Satan then stands on top of the box while demons lift a curtain on the "ten count." When the curtain is dropped on "one," Jesus is no longer in the box, but standing on top. When the angels unlock the box, Satan is inside. It adds a new and powerful element to an old, and probably the most often performed worldwide, human video.

Martial Arts

Consider some of the crisp movements found in the martial arts that are done in unison with the others in their group.

Mime

The art of mime is all about movement. Consider borrowing some of their symbols for emotion, action, or props. However, remember that the movements in a human video still need to be real.

Movies (Silent and Older)

Before movies had sound, an emotion had to be portrayed through movement. Consider watching an old film to see how they portrayed feelings without the use of dialog. This also affected a lot of early movies. Even after sound was introduced, a lot of physical action was still used.

Music Videos

As already mentioned, human video was birthed from the music video, which makes a visual representation of a song. If you can view the music video to the song you want to perform, even better.

Opera

Opera is often sung in other languages such as Italian, and yet many Americans appreciate this art form. Why? Because the story comes through the actors' actions, not just their words.

Determine and Write Your Resolution

As already discussed, your ending is very important to your message. It sends your audience away with an emotion and begs a response. Use thoughtful consideration and prayer when creating this piece of your project.

Does your character become a believer? Find acceptance? Change paths in life? The resolution doesn't always have to be positive, but the message needs to be clear. In DC Talk's "Things of This World," I direct half the actors to choose God while the other half clings to the world. The resolution is solemn for those who meet their evil master in the end, but the meaning is obvious.

Polish the Human Video

Now that you've completed your first draft, it's time to fine-tune your human video. Put it all together and go over it until the performance flows.

Practice in Front of a Mirror

Practicing the motions while looking at your reflection is helpful on many levels. Often the timing may be off or it may not look right, and some rewriting may be in order. It is good to tighten the presentation before you present it to a team. If you don't work out the kinks before you show it to them, you may find yourself — and them — frustrated.

When you are directing, it is often helpful for those learning a human video if you mirror the actors. In other words, do the actions backwards from what you want them to do. If you want them to lean to the left, you lean to the right. That way they are following you. Often aerobic instructors will do this.

Make Any Adjustments That Are Needed

Don't be opposed to changing things at any point in the process. You'll notice I state that several times throughout this book. Even when you begin to practice with your team, some actions may not work the way you had hoped. A good thing to keep in mind is that a human video is a work in progress. I've been doing some of the same human videos for over a decade, and both my team and I still alter things. Don't get frustrated if something isn't working — just change it.

Cast the Human Video and Practice with the Team

When casting, try to consider who is good at emotion and who is good at crisp motion. If you are a new team, this may prove a bit difficult. Something that works for me is playing acting games. This helps me discover different abilities without putting the actors on the spot.

Picking the right person for a role can be crucial. In a story-driven video, emotion is key to grabbing your audience. An actor who can convincingly cry or show passion would be great for this type of role.

An action-driven video, however, takes a different sort of actor. The best people for this sort of human video have the ability to move their bodies in crisp unison. Those who can execute military-type movements well greatly affect the power of what is seen.

Sample Human Video Script (with Lyrics)

Here is one example of how to write a script with lyrics. (This song, "Quality Time," may be found on the CD *Giving All My Praise*. It may be purchased at www.daviddowlen.com.)

Quality Time
By David Dowlen
Copyright © 2005 *Giving All My Praise*
Used by permission.

Characters: Jesus, Person, Four Extras
Set/Props: Couch (Or chairs pushed together), blanket and pillow. You can mime coffeepot, briefcase, coat, watch, and cell phone.
Costumes: Jesus' robe, bathrobe, business jacket, matching shirts (for extras).

1 (EXTRAS start with full back to audience, Stage Right next
2 to couch. PERSON is asleep on the couch, and JESUS is
3 standing behind couch. For full impact, have JESUS mouth
4 the words.)
5
6 Verse 1
7 I woke you up early this
8 morning, *(JESUS taps*
9 *PERSON. PERSON sits up and stretches.)*
10 Hoping you'd spend some time with me. *(JESUS sits on the*
11 *couch next to PERSON, ready for some quality time.*
12 *PERSON ignores him, stands, and pretends to pour a cup of*
13 *coffee.)*
14 Every day you're in a rush — child, when will you see
15 *(PERSON checks watch, now in a rush. Puts on coat, looks*
16 *for a lost shoe, etc., oblivious to JESUS on the couch.)*

How much you mean to me? *(JESUS reaches out to touch PERSON's shoulder. PERSON doesn't notice and picks up a pretend briefcase and checks watch again.)*
And that this is where you should wanna be, *(JESUS puts arms out and walks to PERSON, who pretends to hail a cab.)*
Right here alone — like we used to do, *(JESUS brings left hand flat against chest and points with right hand to couch.)*
Oooh, how I miss my time with you. *(JESUS shakes head sadly as PERSON walks past him and stands with full back to audience.)*
CHORUS
(JESUS stands Center Stage and EXTRAS turn around on "time."

```
X X X X ⎡  ⎤
        |  |
        |  |
           J
```

JESUS and EXTRAS act out whole chorus together unless otherwise noted.)
Time with you is time I treasure, *(From zero position, extend out right pointer and middle finger from hand and touch left outer wrist. Left hand makes a fist, both elbows are slightly pointing toward the audience.)*
Things in life will never measure *(Right arm sweeps up in the air and mimes pouring into the left hand.)*
Up to the precious love I feel for you. *(Look up and cross hands over chest.)*
Don't run and hide, I'm by your side. *(EXTRAS turn and step to the left away from JESUS while bringing their right hands over their heads to cover eyes with the head down. JESUS steps forward to EXTRAS. They go back to zero.)*
It breaks my heart when you put things before me. *(Put fists to chest with pinkies touching [hands look like a heart] and pull them out and away from the chest.)*
I shed my blood and died for you on Calvary, *(Arms sweep out to each side like being on the cross.)*

1	So when you turn your back to me and walk away, *(JESUS*
2	*steps forward and EXTRAS do an about-face so that they*
3	*have full back to audience and then step forward one step.)*
4	You miss the blessings I had for you today. *(JESUS looks*
5	*down at open hands and pretends to pocket the blessings.*
6	*EXTRAS' heads go down on "today.")*
7	
8	*Verse 2*
9	You come home and I'm
10	still here, waiting
11	*(JESUS sits on couch.*
12	*PERSON turns back around and JESUS stands, anxious to*
13	*see PERSON.)*
14	For you to tell me about your day. *(PERSON mimes tossing*
15	*briefcase and looks at watch.)*
16	You hang up your coat — turn on the news — *(PERSON*
17	*mimes tossing coat and turning on the TV.)*
18	And you still ain't noticed
19	how I wait for you,
20	*(PERSON kicks back*
21	*on the couch, takes off*
22	*shoes, yawns. JESUS*
23	*sits on edge of couch, sad.)*
24	For you to get down on your knees and talk to me, *(JESUS*
25	*folds hands, closes eyes, and shakes head.)*
26	And know I kept you from some things you could not see.
27	*(JESUS stands and spans hand out, facing audience.)*
28	Oooh, I hold you safely in the palms of my hands. *(JESUS*
29	*pulls his hands back in, looks at them and moves to*
30	*PERSON's side.)*
31	My love for you — you will never understand. *(JESUS places*
32	*a clawed right hand to chest and pulls it out, then places it*
33	*into PERSON's chest. JESUS shakes head.)*
34	
35	

```
X X X X   ┌─┐
         J   P
```

```
X X X X  │J P│
```

Chapter 3 — Creating a Human Video with *Lyrics*

```
                              ┌─────────────────┐
  CHORUS                      │ X  X  X  X      │
  (JESUS stands Center Stage  │            ┌─ ─┐│
      and  EXTRAS   turn      │            │ P ││
      around on "time" and    │    J       │   ││
      act out the whole chorus together.)  └───┘│
                              └─────────────────┘
```

Time with you is time I treasure, *(Right pointer and middle finger extend out from hand and touch left wrist. Left hand makes a fist. Both elbows are slightly pointing toward the audience.)*

Things in life will never measure *(Right arm sweeps straight out to side and mimes grabbing air. Pulls it to middle of body. Left hand then does the same. Once both hands are in the middle, they open; ACTORS look disappointed at empty hands.)*

Up to the precious love I feel for you. *(Looks up and crosses hands over chest.)*

Don't run and hide, I'm by your side. *(EXTRAS turn away from JESUS while lunging to the left and covering eyes with their right arms. JESUS steps forward to EXTRAS; they go back to zero.)*

It breaks my heart when you put things before me. *(JESUS puts fists to chest with pinkies touching [hands look like a heart] and pulls them out and away from his chest.)*

I shed my blood and died for you on Calvary, *(Arms sweep out to each side like being on the cross.)*

So when you turn your back to me and walk away, *(JESUS steps forward and EXTRAS do an about-face so that they turn full back to audience and then step forward one step.)*

You miss the blessings I had for you today. *(JESUS looks down at open hands and pretends to pocket the blessings.)*

Ad-libs

Some of the blessings that you miss *(JESUS sits on couch by PERSON with*

```
┌──────────────────────┐
│ X  X  X  X   ┌─ ─┐   │
│              │J  P│   │
│              └────┘   │
└──────────────────────┘
```

43

hands cupped as if carrying something and offers it to PERSON.)

Oooh, is when you put me last on your list. *(PERSON puts up finger as if to say, "Just a second," answers his cell phone, shrugs, shakes head, and walks a few steps away.)*

Oooh, how it grieves this heart of mine *(JESUS grabs chest, grieved. He slumps on the couch.)*

For you and me to not have our quality time. *(JESUS puts open right hand out to PERSON, then left arm across abdomen and rests right elbow in left hand and brings right hand to chin.)*

```
X X X X    J
                P
```

CHORUS *(3x)*
(JESUS stands Center Stage and EXTRAS turn around on "time" and act out whole chorus together.)

```
X X X X      P
         J
```

Time with you is time I treasure, *(Right pointer and middle finger extend out from hand and touch left wrist. Left hand makes a fist, both elbows are slightly pointing toward the audience.)*

Things in life will never measure *(Right arm sweeps straight out to side and mimes grabbing air. Pulls it to middle of body. Left hand then does the same. Once both hands are in the middle, they open; ACTORS look disappointed at empty hands.)*

Up to the precious love I feel for you. *(Look up and cross hands over chest.)*

Don't run and hide, I'm by your side. *(EXTRAS turn away from JESUS while lunging to the left and cover eyes with their right arms. JESUS steps forward to EXTRAS, they go back to zero.)*

Chapter 3 — Creating a Human Video with *Lyrics*

It breaks my heart when you put things before me. *(Put fists to chest with pinkies touching [hands look like a heart] and pull them out and away from the chest.)*
I shed my blood and died for you on Calvary, *(Arms sweep out to each side like being on the cross.)*
So when you turn your back to me and walk away, *(JESUS steps forward and EXTRAS do an about-face so that they have full back to audience and then step forward one step.)*
You miss the blessings I had for you today. *(JESUS looks down at open hands and pretends to pocket the blessings.)*

Music Interlude
(PERSON sees Bible on couch, looks around,

X X X X | J P

picks it up and opens it. JESUS sits next to PERSON and together they read, smile, have a good time. Improv or freeze until music stops.)

Chapter 4
Creating a Human Video *without* Lyrics

*"The world is hungry for **real** people and situations. Reality television is popular because you never know what might happen. What makes human video so intriguing is that it isn't performed by professional actors, but rather real people sharing their hearts."*

— Sean Lambert, President and CEO, Youth With A Mission, San Diego/Baja, and author of the human video *The Redeemer*.

So far we've discussed how to prepare a human video using a CD track with lyrics. Now we'll look at how to create your own human video from scratch without the use of words. This is extremely helpful if you have a specific message but can't find a song, or if you're going on a mission trip where the spoken language is something other than English.

Wordless human videos are performed to an instrumental accompaniment only. The participants use motions to portray the emotion *and* the story. Similar to dance, it is important that the movements are grand and comprehensible. Here are several steps to help you create your own video.

Step 1: Determine the Story

As with any story, there are key elements to making the video flow. At the core of every human video, there must be conflict as well as a climax and a resolution. Think of the human video as a moving painting or live novel.

What Is Your Message?

What do you want to get across in your human video? What is the obstacle that your character(s) will face? What is the focus of the pastor's message? What does the audience need to hear? What subject are you passionate about?

What Are Your Five W's?

Who (Audience)
For whom will you perform?
What (Theme)
What is the subject matter of the human video?
Where (Setting)
Where does the human video take place?
When (Time)
When does the play take place both in the setting and in real life? (Sunday church service, Wednesday youth gathering, overseas mission trip, etc.)
Why (Purpose)
What is your intention? (To motivate the church, to preach salvation, to encourage the hurting, etc.)

Where do you find ideas?

Watch Other Human Videos

A great way to generate ideas is to observe others performing and let their efforts spark your own creativity. If you can, find out who is performing a human video in your area and go watch them. Also, some organizations like Youth With A Mission or Drama Source (See Appendix E) offer human videos that you may purchase.

Watch Plays

Observing plays is a great way to get started. Take your journal and write what works and what doesn't. Pay attention to structure. Find the conflict. Get to know the characters.

Observe People

Watching the way people act can help create realistic characters in your script. Sit in public places and write about what you see.

Read

Human videos are stories. Reading can help to inspire ideas. Read plays, short stories, poems, songs, Internet articles, novels, etc.

Consider Personal Experience

The best ideas often come from your own struggles. The passion of your own experience will show through the work and give it depth.

Incorporate Personal Beliefs

In order to convey a message, your beliefs should drive your work.

Be Creative

Let your mind wander and create. Don't hold back, just start jotting down ideas. Some you may finish and others you may not, but something will eventually click.

Recall Sunday School

Do you remember how entertained you were as a kid watching those great flannelgraph stories? Well, the Bible is still full of great, life-altering stories. Any subject you wish to address may be found in the Word.

Step 2: Write the Script

Outline
What is your story baseline? An outline will help you determine how many characters you need, your plot, conflict, climax, and resolution.

What Is Conflict?
Conflict is better described as the "problem." What motivates your characters? What keeps them from their goals? The conflict makes the human video worth watching. Without it, it is simply movement without purpose. All good stories need conflict.

What Is Climax?
The climax is the peak of the problem. It's the point in the human video when all the characters must make a choice — a choice that will determine the outcome.

What Is Resolution?
The resolution is the manner in which the problem is fixed or how the characters will continue to live their lives according to their decisions during the climax. The only time a resolution may not be clear is when the human video is used to complement a sermon.

Create Characters
In every story, you need a protagonist and at least one antagonist. These two characters create conflict. Without them, there is no story.

Protagonist
Character(s) that must *want* something. His or her want causes conflict.

Man vs. Man (Relationships)
This would be a person at odds with another, such as a family member, friend, enemy, etc.

Man vs. Himself (Internal Conflict)
This would be a character that struggles with an addiction, mental problems, letting go, etc.

Man vs. Nature (Elements)
This is a fight against weather (like a hurricane), an animal, disease, etc.

Man vs. God (Spirituality)
This would be a fight against sin and salvation or running from God's will.

A protagonist must appeal to the audience. His or her need must provoke the audience to care. Whether an audience likes the protagonist or not is not the issue, but they must have some sort of connection with him or her.

Antagonist

Usually a stronger character than your protagonist; he, she, or it stands in the way of the protagonist getting what he or she *wants*. (An antagonist doesn't have to be a person. It can be drugs, the world, depression, etc.)

Questions to consider:

How many characters do you want? Who else is needed to make your story work?

This will be influenced by the size of your available team. If you have a large team, but the song only calls for two characters, you can often use the extras to perform the chorus motions without assigning them a part in the actual story — sort of like the back-up dancers at a concert.

Who is your protagonist and what is his or her problem?

Is it a lonely drug addict who needs to find acceptance through Christ? (Evangelism outreach)

Is it a businessman who works too much, neglecting his family and needing to realize how this will impact his future? (Church setting)

Is it a lost teenager who needs to know someone cares? (Youth group)

Who is your antagonist and what is his, her, or its relationship to your protagonist?

Is this a demon, an item, another person, etc.?

What are the details behind your character?
- Who is this person?
- How old is your character?
- What does he or she look like?
- What kind of clothes does he or she wear?
- What is his or her most prominent trait?

- What kind of job does he or she have?
- What kind of hobbies does he or she have on the side?
- What makes him or her really happy?
- What makes him or her really sad?
- What kind of people does he or she like?
- What kind of people does he or she dislike?
- What secrets does he or she have?
- What does he or she want out of life?
- What is his or her main objective?
- What is standing in his or her way from that objective?
- What motivates your character?

(See Appendix B for a more detailed Character Description Worksheet.)

Create a Goal

What is your message and how can you best portray it?
- Is it a story-driven or action-driven video?
- Is it meant to persuade, inform, or ask a question?
- Is your goal evangelism, accompanying a sermon, praise and worship, etc.?

How long do you want your human video to be?

If you're creating your own music, this is open, but if you're counting on pre-recorded music, this is determined. A good human video length is about three to five minutes.

Who can you get to help you?
- Are you musically talented, or do you know someone who can perform the music for you?
- Are you adept at choreography, or is there someone in the church who used to be a dancer or a mime who might have good ideas?
- Do you know anyone who has taught human video before?

Where will your video be performed, and who is your audience?
- Is it a church service or an outreach event?
- What is their age range? Gender? Race? Social situation?

When do you need to be finished with your script?
- Do you have months to work on it, or is it just around the corner? If the deadline is close, you may want prerecorded music.

Develop Structure

A normal play script is all dialog. A human video is all stage directions, but it still has a story. The story is built in three steps:

Beginning (Start of the human video)

This is where you introduce your characters, portray their backgrounds, and establish your setting.

Middle (Rising action)

This is the introduction of difficulties, consequences, change, obstacles, and everything leading up to the climax.

Ending (Includes the climax and the resolution)

Climax (Exciting moment of truth)

It is the highest action and/or the high point of the play, which makes or breaks your "hero(s)." It is the moment in a human video when a choice must be made.

Resolution (What happens after the climatic decision)

The resolution often ties up loose ends and returns order to everyone's life. It can point the way to "happily ever after" or tragedy. Resolution is the result of the choices that were made in the climax.

Unlike a play, in a human video it isn't uncommon for each of the steps to happen in only one scene. For instance, a man may be struggling with binge drinking *(beginning)*. Jesus enters, and the man has to decide between the bottle and Jesus *(middle)*. He finally tosses the bottle and falls at his feet *(climax)*. He is then forgiven and begins to reach out to others *(resolution)*. All of the steps have occurred, and the human video has just started. Maybe there are four other people with similar problems, each with the same outcome. There is a lot of creative freedom in human video. The only thing that is certain is the resolution, which always offers hope to the audience.

Begin to Write

First, write your story in narrative form similar to a short story. This will help you develop the plot and shape your idea. For instance, here is an excerpt from my human video *The Woman* (produced by Youth With A Mission):

The woman sways back and forth like a little girl, clutching her doll. She is so happy. Two of her friends enter and wave. The woman shows them her doll. At first they seemed excited for her, but then one of her friends grabs the doll and they begin to play keep-away. They throw it back and forth over her head. Finally, one of the friends tosses it on the ground and they walk away, gloating as they go.

Once you've written out your story, you then break it down into script form. It looks like this:

WOMAN: *(On the second beat of the music, she enters spinning around, holding the doll out in front of her. She stops turning and begins to sway back and forth, caressing her doll.)*

FRIENDS 1 and 2: *(The FRIENDS enter skipping. They spot the WOMAN and cross to her. They look at her doll for a moment and then begin playing tag with the WOMAN. When the music changes, FRIEND 2 grabs the doll, and both FRIENDS begin to play keep-away. On the fourth time, FRIEND 2 has the doll, he/she throws it on the ground, and they both exit to Stage Left like bratty kids.)*

A human video script is written with directions for action and emotion without any dialog. In a way, writing the wordless human video is similar to writing a short story. The actors don't have words or lyrics in a song to help them understand the vision of the human video; therefore, the script has to explain the story.

Make sure to include the following:
1. *Character prompts* — (Name in uppercase letters, e.g. WOMAN.)
2. *Emotional cues* — (Excited, gloating.)
3. *Musical direction* — (Music changes or after two beats.)
4. *Physical action* — (Sways back and forth.)
5. *Prop handling* — (Clutches a doll.)

Step 3: Choose (or Create) Your Music

Determine if you will write your music, or if you can find music to fit your script. If you write music, you'll have more control over the emotions that are portrayed in the music. In *The Woman,* upbeat music plays when she is happy and sad music plays when something negative happens. When Christ comes into her life at the end, an entirely different score plays.

Step 4: Workshop the Video

Seek out some volunteers to act out your proposed script. The visual aid will help you formulate and tighten ideas. You might even consider videotaping the team before creating the music, for then your composer can create the score to fit the emotions and timing.

Step 5: Revise the Script

Step three could alter your script. If you choose a song that was prerecorded, it may be too long or too short for your script and you may need to cut or add a few steps.

Here are a few things to consider:
- *Be open to critiques.*
- *Workshop the human video with your group to work out the bugs.*
- *Realize it is a work in progress.*

When my team did *The Woman,* we performed it with fifteen people. When I approached Youth With A Mission, they needed the human video to have a cast of less than nine. I knew that if I wanted to publish with them, the project would have to be rewritten, re-taught, and re-filmed. This could have been frustrating, but I understood it was part of the process. A fifteen-person cast wouldn't work for their organization. The attitude in any ministry should always err on the side of flexible. Sometimes you'll have actors quit mid-rehearsal, or maybe a stage will be smaller than the area in which you practiced. In the writer's world, those things that one doesn't want to get rid of are called "little darlings." Don't hold so tightly that your "little darling" ruins the chance to change lives. Whatever the reason, always be willing to let go.

Step 6: List the Props, Costumes, Set, Etc.

Figure out what props, costumes, makeup, set pieces, etc., you will need for your human video and list them. Pay special attention to your props in your stage directions. This includes:
1. Who starts with what prop.
2. Where each prop is located.
3. Where each prop ends up.

Props can really add to a message without words. Different props represent different ideas. (See Chapter 6, "Preparing and Performing a Human Video," for some of these ideas.) Keep in mind that fewer props (and costumes) can make performing in evangelistic and outdoor settings an easier task.

Step 7: Draw the Stage Directions

Sometimes it's helpful to have a drawing of the stage directions for the more visual type of actor. Start with a stage diagram, which usually consists of a box with the words Stage Right (your left), Stage Left (your right), Upstage (toward the back wall), and Downstage (toward the audience). The characters may be portrayed as stick figures, letters, or circles. Each one is numbered, and then arrows show their movement per scene. Some publishing companies like these included, but it is not always necessary.

Step 8: Practice Makes Perfect

As mentioned previously, it is important that your cast practices until each movement is tight. A human video uses muscle memory. The more a person repeats an action, the more likely he or she will automatically do it right the next time. Think about driving home from work in the evenings. Most of the time you probably don't even think about where to turn off; your body just does it. The same will work for human video. There is no such thing as too much practice.

Step 9: Prepare to Perform

Don't forget to pray. It is your greatest weapon. Don't go out there without tapping into this power source. An hour before going on, I always have my team sit in a circle to discuss how they hope to minister through the use of the human video. In addition, be sure to stretch out and exercise.

Step 10: Present the Piece

Perform your human video for the glory of God alone! Let him be your motivation.

Sample Project
(Using the steps listed above)

(See Appendix A, "Creating Your Wordless Video," to figure out your own project.)

Message: Running the Race
1 Corinthians 9:24-25

"You know that many runners enter a race, and only one of them wins the prize. So run to win! Athletes work hard to win a crown that cannot last, but we do it for a crown that will last forever."

The 5 W's:
Who: (Audience) — The Church.
What: (Theme) — Perseverance in the Christian life.
Where: (Setting) — Racetrack.
When: (Time) — Set in any time, Wednesday Night Service.
Why: (Purpose) — To encourage Christians in their faith.

Basic Story Line:
The Runner starts his race running with enthusiasm. When we are born, we all begin running the race of life. We start strong, but before we know it, the world begins weighing us down. For the Runner, education, sex, substance abuse, competition, etc., all became a weight that kept him from being able to move forward and meet the Savior. But when he allowed the Holy Spirit to direct him, he was able to make it to the finish line and into the arms of Christ.

Outline:
1. Runner begins running strong toward Jesus at the finish line.
2. Philosopher comes in and hands the Runner a stack of books, implying that the only way to get stronger in one's faith is to read lots of books.
3. This makes the Runner run slower.
4. A worldly girl enters and gives him a beer and flirts with him, distracting him from Jesus.
5. The Runner runs slower.
6. A discouraging person enters, pushes the Runner, and

knocks him down.
7. The Runner falls and gives up.
8. The Holy Spirit comes alongside the Runner and takes the books and beer away.
9. The Holy Spirit hands him a pocket-size Bible and a bottle of Living Water.
10. The Runner takes a drink, stands, and begins running again.
11. Runner runs through a tape and into Jesus' arms.

Conflict:
The distractions of the world, the feelings of insecurity, and wanting to give up on one's faith become the Runner's crises.

Climax:
When the Runner falls and wants to give up.

Resolution:
When the Runner gets back up and runs into Jesus' arms.

Characters:
Protagonist — Runner
Antagonist(s) — Philosopher, Girl, and Discourager
They all represent the world that distracts and discourages the Christian.
Other Characters — Jesus, Holy Spirit, and tape holders

Music:
My husband will create the music after my team acts out the parts. We will videotape the team, and he will create a sound to match their emotions.

Props:
Brown bottle
Bottle of water with "Living Water" label (In English or Spanish)
Streamer
Big Christian Books (Doesn't matter what they are)
Small Bible

Costumes:
Runner — Running attire
Philosopher — College robe or sweatshirt
Girl — Cute dress
Discourager — Leather jacket
Jesus — White robe with blue sash
Holy Spirit — White robe
Tape holders — Running attire

Sample Wordless Human Video Script

The Runner
Music by Richard Mendoza
A human video about the race we all run and the eternal prize that awaits us.

Cast of Characters
Runner — Running the race of life. (M)
Philosopher — Believes education is the way to God. (M/F)
Girl — Represents sex and partying. (F)
Discourager — Represents the people in life who tell us we're not good enough or that we can't make it. (M/F)
Holy Spirit — The inner voice that encourages us and helps us find our way to Jesus. (M/F)
Jesus — Our Savior. (M)

Note: You will need a couple of people to hold a streamer in front of JESUS. This could even be people from the audience.

1	(All ACTORS begin full back to audience. Music begins slowly.)
2	**JESUS:** (Steps to the finish line Upstage Right and holds out
3	hands.)
4	**RUNNER:** (He turns around, kneels, prays, and asks JESUS to
5	come into his life. He stands and stretches. He then starts to
6	run in place. He faces diagonally toward JESUS, open
7	enough that the audience can see him.)
8	(Music changes.)
9	**PHILOSOPHER:** (He or she runs up next
10	to the RUNNER with a pile of books.
11	The PHILOSOPHER looks at him and
12	then begins piling books into the
13	RUNNER's hands, as if to say he
14	won't make it in his Christian walk
15	without education. He or she then exits.)

```
P   G   D

            R

J
```

Chapter 4 — Creating a Human Video without *Lyrics*

1   *(Music changes.)*
2   **RUNNER:** *(RUNNER begins to feel loaded down and has a little*
3   *trouble running. He tries to look at the books but ends up*
4   *getting disoriented.)*
5   *(Music changes.)*
6   **GIRL:** *(She runs in with a beer and begins*
7   *flirting with RUNNER. She runs*
8   *behind him, tracing her finger along*
9   *his back.)*
10   **RUNNER:** *(He smiles.)*
11   **GIRL:** *(She snuggles up to him on his right side, forcing him to*
12   *focus on her and no longer on JESUS. She offers him the*
13   *beer.)*
14   **RUNNER:** *(He shakes his head.)*
15   **GIRL:** *(She smiles and winks at him.)*
16   **RUNNER:** *(He smiles and takes the beer. He drinks and begins*
17   *to run slower.)*
18   **GIRL:** *(Waves and runs past RUNNER.)*
19   *(Music changes.)*
20   **RUNNER:** *(He follows her with his eyes and trips. He almost*
21   *falls, but recovers. He's getting really tired now.)*
22   *(Music changes.)*
23   **DISCOURAGER:** *(Enters and begins*
24   *running circles around the RUNNER,*
25   *taunting him. He or she pushes him,*
26   *spins him around, and yells at him,*
27   *then trips him.)*
28   *(Music changes to the sound of heartbeats.)*
29   **RUNNER:** *(Falls.)*
30   **DISCOURAGER:** *(Runs off.)*
31   **RUNNER:** *(Broken, he gives up.)*

1   **HOLY SPIRIT:** *(Enters and takes books*
2   *and hands RUNNER a small Bible.*
3   *Takes the beer and hands RUNNER a*
4   *bottle of "Living Water." He/She offers*
5   *to help RUNNER up and motions to*
6   *finish line.)*

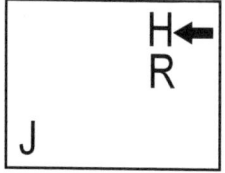

7   **RUNNER:** *(Reads from the Bible and starts to stand. Takes a*
8   *drink of water and gets up with Holy Spirt running*
9   *alongside. RUNNER starts to run when music changes.)*
10 **RUNNER:** *(Begins running again. Takes a*
11 *drink from water and starts to run*
12 *faster. He runs through streamer finish*
13 *line and into JESUS' arms and freezes*
14 *as music ends.)*

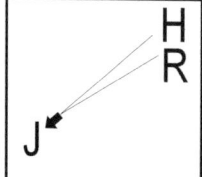

Chapter 5
Directing a Human Video

"In real life, actions speak louder than words. The beauty of human video and mime is that one tends to listen more intently when words aren't used. It is quite a phenomenon!"

— David Willsey, Professional Mime, *A Mime and His Maker*

Directing a human video can be quite the task. It's more than handing an actor a script and telling him or her to perform. It involves sharing a vision, directing emotion, and training in choreography.

Directing Human Video in General

In any human video you can expect to share the vision, cast the roles, block the action, and practice. Here is a list of ideas to help you along your journey.

Listen

Ask everyone involved to listen to the song without instruction. This gives them the chance to hear it the way the audience will hear it. I often tell my team to shut their eyes and just listen to the words.

Share

Share your vision for the video. You want your team to understand the mission and to adopt it as their own. Explain the theme to them, tell them why you chose the song, where you plan to perform it, and what you plan to achieve. Explain the story or stories in the song and the characters that you plan to use. For example, if *Jesus, My Friend* was your human video, you might talk about how three people are struggling to put God first. You'd then explain each character's personal struggle and their obstacle (antagonist). Maybe one guy only gives God an hour each morning, another only gives God Sundays, and the last person, only holidays.

Cast

Cast the human video. Figure out how many actors you need for the human video and then cast according to believability and their skills.

One of the best things that anyone ever did for me was to give me a chance. I have kept that in my mind for years. Just because a person isn't good at emotions doesn't mean he or she doesn't have a place in human video. That's the beauty of human video. There's a place for everyone. When casting a *story-driven* script, consider these things:

- Who can cry?

- Who can visually express passion?
- Who is good at showing anger or delight?

Actors who are good at emoting are great for story-driven human videos because their believability in a role makes the audience sympathize with their plight and therefore experience the same emotion. Often it tugs at the heartstrings. This is important when you are performing a human video that begs a response.

When casting an *action-driven* human video, you are looking for different characteristics:
- Who is good at motions?
- Who can implement crisp, military-type movements?
- Who is good at keeping in sync with others?

Actors who are good at precision movements or have a background in dance are often great in an action-driven video.

 *If you have a large team, consider having some of your newer actors, or someone who struggles with the art, act out the chorus. Choruses are typically shorter than the verses and repeat several times, thus giving them more experience.*

Teach

Teach the chorus first. Since the chorus, as already mentioned in earlier chapters, is the part of the song that will be done the most often and by the majority of actors, teach it first. It will get both your actors and the process moving.

Block

Block the different scenes. Explain each scene so your team has an idea about how the human video will flow. I often play the music and act out an entire video for the team first. If you're not comfortable doing that, you may just talk them through it.

Learn

Learn the movements and then use the music. Place your people on the stage in their particular order and position. Walk them through the human video a little bit at a time. Try not to move on until you think they've grasped the scene. If you move on too soon, you'll most likely have to teach the first part again. When you think they're ready, run the scene with the music.

Practice

Practice, practice, practice. There is no such thing as too much practice. Your team may grow tired of the song by the time it's over, but they'll feel good when they nail the video in their place of ministry.

Adjust

Adjust when needed. As already stated, a human video is a work in progress. Change it until it works for your team.

Tune-up

Fine tune the different movements to match everyone else. Once the team knows the video well, have them perform it step by step without the music to make sure everyone is moving in unison. For example: Are their hands all chest level? Are their upraised arms straight up or at an angle? Are their feet apart or together?

 *I often have the cast face each other and determine where their hands should be for each line of the song.*

Pray

Pray, perform, and let God work. Once you've arrived at the night of your performance, it is too late to worry. Pray for God's anointing and peace, and for his will to be done. Then let go.

Training a Specific Project — Do's and Don't's

Admit Flaws

DON'T be afraid to admit that something is not working. The message is the most important part — not one's ego. If it isn't working, change it. Many times a move looks great in your head or in the mirror, but when ten people are performing it, it just doesn't work. A human video can often be like a puzzle. You just have to find the perfect fit.

Realize Its Purpose

DO realize that this is ministry, not a performance. Everything doesn't have to be perfect; the message just has to be clear. I will take a mediocre actor with heart over a trained thespian with attitude any day.

Always Pray
DO bathe your human video in prayer.
"... Always pray by the power of the Spirit ..."
(Ephesians 6:18).

I know I've mentioned prayer already, and you can be assured I will mention it again, because it is the Holy Spirit who penetrates the hearts of an audience. It is the Lord who will enable your team to execute a flawless performance. It is for him that this book even exists.

About five years ago, my team was scheduled to perform for the first time ever in the main service at our church. We had been practicing all day, but the performance was getting worse. I was watching from the sound booth when one of the girls yelled up, "We need to pray." I thought she said, "We need a break." Well, I about lost it. "What do you mean, 'take a break'?" I said. "That was awful." The team laughed as she annunciated her words, "I said, 'we need to pray.'" She was right. We prayed, and they nailed the human video every time after that. That moment taught my team the power of prayer. If we never ministered again, I am grateful for that experience.

Prayer must be your number one element. It will get you to your goal of ministering to others. Going into a ministry setting, we don't know the individual hearts in the audience. Only God does, and only he has the ability to change lives. Therefore, he needs to be invited into every performance.

Utilize Your Body
DO have the actors use every part of their body to tell the story. There are no spoken lines in human video. The whole story is told through movement. Emotion and/or message has the ability to come through that movement when performed one hundred percent. I often tell my group, "You will only look silly if you give it half-effort." When they give it their all, no matter if they're in a monkey costume or a suit and tie, the audience will pay attention. (See Appendix D, "Suggestions for Expressing Emotion through Body Language," for suggestions.)

Also, be sure to exaggerate motions on-stage. Make them BIG, so viewers in the back row can see an exchange as clearly as those in the front row. Big motions, overextended, are always a good thing.

Use Energy

DON'T use lazy movements. I am constantly telling my team to be "crisper." Crisp movements look wonderful, and they also convey to the audience a full commitment to the project.

Some human videos have more natural motions (story-driven), while others may be military-type actions done in unison (action-driven). When performing the action-driven video, sloppy movements can prevent success. A way to achieve crisp movement is to feel tension in the arms, head, and legs. I often stand back and have my team perform the piece without music. I stop them at every line to see that all their limbs have tension.

Practice

DO practice often. Practicing before performing a human video can't be underestimated. It takes time to get it right. Unlike a play script, the song in a human video keeps going, even if a person messes up. The more the team practices, obviously the better they'll be.

Action-driven human videos usually take more time, because everyone has to be synchronized. On average, we practice action-driven human videos twelve to eighteen hours before performing them. A story-driven human video is usually more about emotion than motions. Therefore, my team can often learn one in a couple of hours. The number of practice sessions you need to schedule depends on the experience of your team and the kind of video you plan to undertake.

Know the Lyrics

DO know the lyrics well. It is important to really know the words to the song — to anticipate the line coming up, not the one being performed. If an actor thinks about the movement as the words are being sung, he or she will probably be late in its execution.

I often give the song to my team members to take home. Knowing the lyrics is half the battle, so when we get together, our practice is more about memorizing the movement since they already know the song.

Passion
DO use emotion and passion. Human video is all about the range of feeling. It is powerful and stirring. If the actors show that emotion, the audience will be pulled in and the message will be strong. Even in action-driven human videos, there is a passion that comes through.

Personalize the Ministry
DO encourage the actors to personalize the ministry. I strongly encourage directors to spend time with team members discussing how a given song touches them and relates to them and/or someone they know. This connection to the song helps the ministry to become personal and often ensures a stronger performance. Human video is a powerful tool. It is a sermon of sorts. Like an effective preacher; the actors need to care about the message. You wouldn't want a pastor to get up in the pulpit without a belief in his topic. The same should be true of the people acting out the human video. Before every performance, I ask my team to explain what the human video means to them and why they think it is important.

Create an Alternative
DO have a backup plan. I can't tell you how many times I've had someone get sick or cancel before a performance. It is a good idea to create a version of your human video with a smaller cast in mind. It may not be ideal, but it will often work. Know what your maximum and minimum sizes will be.

Perfecting the Finished Video

Human video is about using the body. Here are several tips to help your actors improve their movement.

Have Motivation for All Movement
Have the actors move in a way that makes sense to the story, the scene, their characters, their mood, etc. For example, it isn't enough for an actor to move just to get out of the way of another actor, but it is enough to have him or her move to grab a prop or because he or she might be angry with another character. If an

actor needs to move, give him or her an emotion and/or reason to travel to another position. Even when an actor's back is to the audience, there should be a reason why he or she is leaving the scene.

Avoid Nervous Movement

Nervous movement distracts the audience from the message. Avoid anything that is inconsistent with one's character, such as:
- Shifting from one foot to the other
- Bouncing off toes or swaying
- Playing with clothes or props
- Flicking or touching hair
- Wringing hands
- Biting lips, smiling, twitching, etc.
- Anything out of character

Discourage Showing Back to the Audience

This is important for two reasons: 1. In human video, an actor is considered off-stage when the actor's back is to the audience. 2. The audience can no longer see the actor's expression and feels shut out from what the actor is doing or experiencing.

Create All Movements to Reflect the Character

The actor's movements should reflect the personality and mood of his or her character. Make sure that the motions the individual is executing make sense to the audience.

Consider the Emotions of Characters When Entering And Exiting

This must be portrayed in the pace, the way they push the door, etc. If they are upset, they'd exit with energy. If they are scared, they'd enter timidly.

Remember to Direct All Areas of the Body

The written stage directions may only consider the arms and feet, but the position of the eyes, hands, toes, hips, back, elbows, etc., all affect the way a character or motion appears. When breaking down a human video, be sure to look at the plane of every motion. Do you want her looking at the floor when she turns around? Do you want his elbows level with his chest when he is miming holding a Bible? Every action requires a full inspection.

Chapter 5 — Directing a Human Video

What Is Wrong with This Picture?

If you were directing this team, what would you change to tighten this performance? Examine the picture closely before turning the page.

1. Focal Point — Where are they looking? **Notice they are all looking in different directions. In a group human video, it is important to establish the actors' focal point.**

2. Arm Angle — Where are they pointing? **Observe each arm. Notice how they are all pointing at different angles.**

Chapter 5 — Directing a Human Video

3. *Hand Position — What are their hands doing?* Look carefully and you'll see that one hand is flat on the floor while some fingers are angled out. The hands in the air are also inconsistent. Some are cupped, others are flat. Some thumbs are out while others aren't.

4. *Leg Position — Where should their legs be?* They are clearly not together. One girl has her left knee on the ground, one guy has both knees up, and the majority have their right legs on the ground.

It is so important to study every part of the body. Break down each scene one line at a time, and make sure everyone knows where each body part should be at all times.

The reason this particular human video looks sloppy is due to insufficient direction. I only told my actors to act out a particular scene from DC Talk's "Things of This World" — nothing more. They remembered the gist of the scene, but directors always need to remind a group about the proper limb placement. Think of dress rehearsals as "body checks."

Every Motion Should Be Ten Times Bigger Than Real Life

When performing on-stage, every action must be big enough for each member of the audience to discern what is happening. Therefore, when an actor pantomimes opening a Bible and turning the pages, he should imagine a large book, like a family Bible, rather than a pocket-size version. Make sure even the nearsighted person in the back row catches every movement.

Use Tension in the Limbs When Performing

When performing the chorus of a story-driven human video or when performing an action-driven human video, always maintain tension in the arms and legs. This crisp movement looks sensational to the audience, while the alternative looks lazy and weak.

Don't Back Down from "Stupid" Motions

My friend and human video veteran Jacob Ballard once said, "If you don't feel stupid, you're probably not doing it right." There is some truth to this. If an actor half expresses an action, the motion might look stupid, but if an actor gives it his or her all, the passion and conviction will overshadow anything dumb. The actors need to push the movements one hundred percent.

Always Step with the Right Foot

Train your team to automatically begin marching with the right foot. This is important for two reasons:

1. There is no second-guessing; the team always knows the right foot comes first and they will move in unison.
2. This is true to military style, so if cadence is ever called, they will be on the correct foot.

Mastering the About-face
Keep hands straight at the side. Wear slick-soled shoes. Place the right big toe about one inch behind the left foot. At the same time, lift up on the ball of the left foot. Pivot to the right 180 degrees on the right toe and the left ball at the same time. You know you've done it right when both feet end up in the shape of a V, the heels touching, without wobbling or toppling over.

Chapter 6
Preparing and Performing a Human Video

"With human video mere lines on a page become caustic elements infused with life, as common words spring into action and stir the heart, awaken the mind, and rouse the soul. Human video is not just a tool for teaching; it is a tool for reviving hearts and calling them to action. I have been deeply stirred — and often shaken — by every human video I've seen. Human video makes everything come to life."

— Steve Babbitt, Senior Pastor, Spring Valley Community Church

Before you "go," you need to be on your mark and then get set. Here are some preparation tips to ensure a successful performance that is as glitch-free as possible.

Purchase Extra Tracks

Always take additional copies of the songs with you. A scratched or lost CD can cause a lot of tension and has the potential to ruin a performance. The Enemy would love nothing more than to keep your team from ministering. In my experience, if it can go wrong, he just might make it happen. My advice is to be prepared.

 *Rehearse with one copy and use another copy for the actual performance.*

Discuss Sound Needs

Mark the track number or put a copy of the song on a CD for the sound person. If you're doing more than one song, you may also give him or her visual cues about when to play each track. Decide if you want the actors to enter with the song already playing or to have it start when some or all of your team is lined up. Communicate with the sound person about the human video and your expectations for the music.

Obtain the Costumes

Figure out what costumes you will need for each human video. Oftentimes in action-driven human videos, matching shirts and/or hats looks good. The truth is, human video does not require a lot of costumes. Sometimes just the symbol, color of the shirt, or a taped-on sign is sufficient.

Costume Suggestions:
Jesus or God — White robe or shirt
Satan or demons — Black robe, cape, and/or shirt
Business person — Suit jacket/glasses
Bible characters — Robes or era costumes

Adam and Eve — Ivy pinned to clothes
Homeless person — Flannel or camouflage
Sinner — Black clothes
Doctor — Smock, robe, or white shirt (with letters M.D.)
Cult member — Ankh or crystal necklace
Christian — Cross necklace or white shirt

Purchase the Props

Figure out what props you will need and collect them. You should also discuss who will have which prop, what are the hand-offs, etc. When you perform a video with many props, consider having some in pockets, on the ground, in a trunk, etc. I often suggest that my team wear pants and shirts with pockets. If that isn't possible, sometimes putting props in the waistband of an actor's pants can work too.

Prop Suggestions:
Partier (Alcohol) — Brown root beer bottle
   (without the wrapper)
Partier (Drugs) — Kid's medicine dropper or
   white twisted drawing paper
Businessman — Cell phone or glasses
Homeless person — Brown bag
Sin — Black cloth or chains
Redemption — White cloth or broken chains
Spiritual death — Dried tree branches
Life — Roses
Teenager — Binder or backpack
Kid — Doll or stuffed animal
Christian — Bible

Props in human video are simple. They are used primarily as a symbol to identify a situation or character.

Practice the Entrances and Exits

Discuss and practice entrances and exits. If it's an action-driven video, you may want to march in. In a story-driven video, you may want your actors to enter as the story unfolds. If they're entering through the audience, consider how many aisles there are and how long each one is. You must also decide if the actors are to march in a straight line or veer off to the sides of the stage. If it is a story-driven video, are they staying on-stage the whole time with their backs to the audience, or are they entering as the action unfolds? Remember, the full back to the audience is considered the same as being off-stage.

Determine the Lighting

Let your lighting technician know if you want any special lighting. This could include:
- Starting in the dark
- Spotlights
- Color gels
- Fading to black or sudden blackout

Note: If you're on the road at a guest church, you may have to go with their light setup. Be flexible, just in case.

Block the Stage

If you've been practicing somewhere else, make sure you block out the human video on the stage before the actual performance. A smaller stage than you practiced on or different entrances than you're used to can alter the human video's effectiveness. For instance, my team once went to an outreach event where we had to perform our ten-person human video on the back of a trailer. The minute we walked on the lot, I knew we were in trouble. I asked the guy in charge if we could have a few minutes to block it out. It's a good thing we did, too. If we had proceeded as practiced, my team could have fallen off the edge before the end of the first scene.

For some action-driven videos, you may want to mark a person's position with tape. This helps the team look uniform and avoids the possibility of accidentally hitting each other. The actors should perform some of the more expansive movements next to each other to determine how far apart they should be when performing. An arm's length is good for human videos that are staggered, but if the actors are in a line, consider two arm lengths.

Tell the actors to place their arms out until they either touch the other actor's fingertips or shoulder. Stand back and make sure all actors may be seen in the "windows." Windows are the openings that keep any actors from being upstaged. When you feel good about the actors' placement, place a piece of tape or a thumbtack under their right toes to mark their spots.

Set Up or Explain the Message

Sometimes a human video needs an introduction, a tie-in to the sermon, or an altar call. It isn't a bad idea to outline some thoughts about the human video and be prepared to say something. Some organizations have a firm belief that no human video should be performed without an explanation. My personal thought is that if the human video is strong enough, no explanation is necessary, but then an altar call is almost always a good idea.

Prepare Spiritually and Physically

Human video is about ministry and touching lives, so preparing the spiritual heart is important through a time of prayer and worship. But human video is also a physical art similar to aerobics. Muscles will get sore, especially if there is any kneeling or lunges. Have the team stretch out before practice and performances with the following:

Suggested Warm-Up Exercises
- Breathe in deeply and exhale slowly.
- Shake out hands, then arms, and then legs.
- Raise arms over head into a stretch.
- Buckle to the floor and then come back up slowly, rolling the shoulders and making sure to bend the knees.
- Stretch right arm over head while leaning to the left.
- Stretch left arm over head while leaning to the right.
- Lunge to the right.
- Lunge to the left.
- Lean neck to the right, then left.
- Place balls of feet on floor and point toes skyward.
- Swing the legs loosely side to side.

- Lift right leg and turn ankle in a circular motion.
- Lift left leg and turn ankle in circular motion.
- Breathe in deeply and exhale slowly.

 *Muscle isolation is a great way to warm up and ease pre-performance jitters. Ask the actors to lie on the ground and close their eyes. Put a worship CD on in the background. Then tell them to tighten and relax each muscle in their bodies, starting with their toes and working up to their heads.*

Discuss, Evaluate, and Record

After each performance, it's a good idea to discuss the performance. My team and I often talk about how the video went, what we could have done better, and what we would do differently the next time. If we make any changes to the human video, I record this on my typed script and save it for the next time. You might also consider videotaping a production for review, discussion, and historical value.

Chapter 7
Publishing a Human Video

"Human video combines the power of music and the imagery of choreography. This is a winning combination that offers a powerful potential."

— Bruce Grecco, Worship and Arts/Associate Pastor, Faith Chapel

If God gives you a wordless human video that can be used globally for God's kingdom, why not publish it? Should you consider attempting to publish it, include these in your presentation:
1. Workbook
2. Training DVD
3. Music CD
4. Prop Kit

Create the Workbook

The workbook gives the director and actors a written piece to follow when learning the details of a human video. Be sure to write an introduction, a definition of human video, any director's notes, the story line, the cast of characters, any props or costumes needed, the setup, the script, and any illustrations, diagrams, and/or pictures.

Introduction

The introduction should include the human video's theme and the purpose. Think of your introduction as an abstract — a short description of your project that encourages a person to read on.

Example of an Introduction:

Temptation is a human video about one man's mission to find meaning in life. He tries to find happiness in money, alcohol, and love, but only finds despair. Then he meets a Christian who introduces him to Jesus Christ.

This human video was created to use as an evangelistic tool.

Human Video Definition

Since human video is still a new concept for some people and is performed by evangelism teams around the world, include a detailed definition of human video. (See Chapter 1, "Human Video Defined.")

Director's Notes

The director's notes are written to the person who is going to be instructing the actors. This includes the number of cast members needed, the focus, the message, etc. I also suggest giving the director some pointers on how to teach your script to others.

Example of Director's Notes:
- Watch the human video and learn it yourself.
- Read the notes to clarify any questions.
- Cast the parts according to the people on your team.
- Gather the team to watch the video.
- Follow the step-by-step portion of the video.
- Ask the team to perform each portion after watching that section.

Story Line

Write out the basic story line scene by scene. This gives the publisher, the director, and the actors a good idea of the scope of this particular human video. Think of it as a synopsis similar to the short description found on the back cover of a book. (See Chapter 4, "Creating a Human Video *without* Lyrics.")

Cast of Characters

List each character with a short bio. Make sure you define the gender, age, and personality. Include any details that will help the actor understand the character and how he or she relates to the story.

Example:
JOHN *(M, 16)* — *Lonely teenager looking for acceptance.*
TEMPTATION *(F, 16)* — *Sultry girl who pushes the world's agenda.*
CHRISTIAN *(M, 16)* — *Kind guy who loves the Lord.*
JESUS *(M)* — *The Lord and Savior.*

Prop Kit

Some publishers or organizations may prefer to include props with the human video. In the script, you'll want to list each item that is included in the kit. If some props aren't included in the kit but are needed for the human video, list them separately. If you decide against including a prop kit, just list all the props that will be needed.

Example of Prop Kit:
Prop Kit includes — Sunglasses, hanky, and fake money
Props not included — Bible and brown bottle

Costumes
List costumes and who will be wearing them.
Example of Costumes:
All actors, except Jesus, wear matching shirts.
Jesus may wear a robe or a white shirt.

Setup
Explain what the set will look like, how the actors will stand as the human video begins, and where the props are dispersed.
Example of Setup:
There is one chair in the middle of the stage. The ACTORS start in a horizontal line, behind the chair, with their backs to the audience. JOHN holds the bottle. TEMPTATION wears the sunglasses and has the money in her back pocket. CHRISTIAN holds the Bible. JESUS has the hanky crumpled in his hand.

Script
Write your script using the directions found in Chapter 3, "Creating a Human Video *with* Lyrics."

When preparing a manuscript to send to a publisher, be sure to use:
- Times New Roman or Courier font
- Twelve-point type in black ink
- Double spacing
- 1" - 1.25" margins
- Header with your name and phone number
- Page numbers, starting at page 2

 *Because this is a music-based human video, you may consider putting musical cues in the script as well.*

Illustrations, Diagrams, and Pictures
It is always helpful to have visual representations of the different movements in the script. Consider including some illustrations, diagrams, or pictures. You can take these with a digital camera, draw them, and/or scan them. Make sure that any computer images are a jpg or tiff, CMYK, 300 dpi or higher. Find out from the publisher if they want you to include them in the body of the text or on a disk.

Prepare the Packet

Music

Make sure to have the *original* music that you've created copied onto a CD. Check the CD before sending it to confirm that it works. It may be used in the final production of your product, so be certain it is a high-quality product.

Training DVD

The training DVD has three parts:
1. Introduction
2. Human video performance
3. Training of the human video

Introduction

This is where you explain your vision, what the project is, and what the director and actors can expect. You can tape yourself, or you can request that someone do it for you. It should be under a minute in length.

Human Video Performance

Tell the actors to act out the human video straight through with the music. If there are any mistakes, tape it again. This may be used in the final product, so do your best to make it a clean performance.

Training

Tape each scene without music. Read the script that you've already created, and instruct the actors to follow each movement as it is written and at a slow pace. Then, at the end of each scene, ask the actors to act out that scene in real time to music. This is a great chance to see if your script works. If you see a flaw, keep taping with the change and fix the script later.

Prop Kit

Consider the cost to the publisher when deciding what props to include in your kit. The cost of the props will affect the price of the final product to the consumer. For this reason, keep the props simple and cost-effective. When I buy a kit, I try to keep the amount under ten dollars. Some props that are readily available, such as a Bible, may be listed in the workbook as "not provided."

When you have your props, make sure they fit into a plastic box with a lid (about 7" x 11 1/2"). If a prop doesn't fit, consider changing it or deleting it.

Send the Project

Once you've prepared your script, taped your DVD, and collected your prop kit, you're ready to market it to publishers and/or evangelism training schools. Here are the steps you'll need to follow in order to publish your human video:

Step 1: Do Your Homework

Find out what organizations use or publish drama. It would be a waste of your (and their) time and money to send a proposal to a company that only publishes devotionals. A good source for locating publishing companies that are interested in drama is Sally Stuart's *Christian Writer's Market Guide*. There are also evangelistic organizations that sell human videos as well. (See "Human Video Resources" in Appendix E.) You might also contact Christians In Theater Arts at www.cita.org to see if they are aware of any organizations that sell human videos.

Step 2: Send a Proposal

Never send a whole packet without permission. Write a proposal that explains what you've created, for whom it is intended, and what is included.

In every correspondence, always include a cover letter. In order to make it more personal, try to obtain the acquisition editor's name. If it is your first contact with that publisher, summarize why you'd like a moment of their time. If it is a response to their interest, then remind them of that request.

If a company accepts correspondence via e-mail, be sure to place the proposal in the body of the e-mail and also attach it. This fail-safe plan ensures that they will be able to read the proposal in the manner they prefer.

Chapter 7 — Publishing a Human Video

PROPOSAL

Name:	*John Doe*
Address:	*1234 Main Street*
	Bermuda Triangle, CA 99999
Phone:	*(555) 555-1234*
E-mail:	*admin@xxxxxxxx.com*
Title:	*My Friend Forgives*
Format:	*Human Video with Training Workbook,*
	Prop Kit, and DVD
Purpose:	*Evangelism*
Verse:	*"My friend, your sins are forgiven"*
	(Luke 5:20).
Short Summary:	*Three people are hurting ...*
	(No more than fifty words.)
Short Bio:	*John Doe is a drama director ...*
	(No more than fifty words.)

Step 3: SASE

Always send a Self-Addressed Stamped Envelope with your packet. This is an envelope that is addressed to you with the correct postage, and it is used for the publishing company to respond to you. For the proposal, send a letter-size envelope, and for your entire project, send the appropriate packing.

The Whole Kit and Caboodle

If the company responds with interest, you can send them the script and DVD. You may ask if they'd prefer having the whole kit up front, or if they'd prefer just receiving the script at that time. When they're ready for it, send them the whole packet with the DVD, prop kit, musical CD, etc. Be sure to include a cover letter that reminds the publisher that they have asked for your project.

Be patient. Publishing is a lengthy process. Allow three months to a year for a response. If a year passes without a response, you may contact the company with a polite letter to see if they are still interested. Never call them. Only e-mail if they prefer or make contact with you first.

Appendices

"[Human video is] taking an idea, philosophy, or truth [and] presenting it in such a way as to affect the target audience artistically, intellectually, and most important — emotionally. They need to feel they are involved."

— Jes Shriver, Senior High Youth Drama Leader,
Abundant Life Foursquare Church

Appendix A
Creating Your Wordless Video Worksheet

(Use the steps listed in Chapter 4.)

Story —

Message: _____

Verse: _____

Who: (Audience) _____

What: (Theme) _____

Where: (Setting) _____

When: (Time) _____

Why: (Purpose) _____

Outline —

_____
_____
_____
_____
_____
_____
_____

Conflict: _____

Climax: _____

Resolution: _____

Basic Story Line: _____

_____
_____

Appendices

Characters —
Protagonist(s): _____

Antagonist(s): _____

Other Characters: _____

_____

Music —

_____

Props —

_____

_____

_____

_____

Costumes —

_____

_____

_____

_____

Appendix B
Character Descriptions for the Actor

Personality
1. What kind of personality does he or she have?
2. If you could see inside his or her head — what would he or she be thinking?
3. What are his or her defining characteristics?
4. What traits differ from the other characters in the video?
5. How does your character act like you? Differ from you?
6. What can you pull from your own life that will help you with this character?
7. What is going to be the toughest thing for you when you play this character?
8. What motivates your character?
9. What does the audience need to believe about your character?
10. Where would you most likely find your character, and what would he or she be doing?

Body
1. How does your character stand? Walk? Sit?
2. What physical motion does he or she frequently make? (For example, a nervous tic.)

Overall Description
1. If you had to describe your character to a friend, how would you depict his or her personality?
2. What help do you need to become this character?

Appendix C
Human Video Song Suggestion List

Below is a list of songs that I have used to successfully direct human videos. I hope some of them will help you as you get started ministering in human video.

Some of the older songs may be difficult to track down. You might try searching on the Internet or on sites like eBay.com or Amazon.com.

1. THEME: Christian Love
    SONG: "If We Are the Body "
    ARTIST: Casting Crowns
        CD: *Casting Crowns*

2. THEME: Compassion/Ministry
    SONG: "Broadway"
    ARTIST: Sherry Youngward
        CD: *Faces, Memories, and Places*

3. THEME: Easter/Passion
    SONG: "I Am"
    ARTIST: Various
        CD: *Hero, the Rock Opera*

4. THEME: Easter/Passion
    SONG: "Secret Ambition"
    ARTIST: Michael W. Smith
        CD: *The First Decade: 1983-1993*

5. THEME: End Times
    SONG: "People Get Ready"
    ARTIST: Crystal Lewis
        CD: *People Get Ready*

6. THEME: Forgiveness/Gifting
   SONG: "In Return"
   ARTIST: Crystal Lewis
      CD: *Beauty for Ashes*

7. THEME: Forgiveness/God's Love
   SONG: "When God Ran"
   ARTIST: Shaded Red
      CD: *Red Revolution*

8. THEME: Freedom from Sin
   SONG: "Remember These Chains"
   ARTIST: Steven Curtis Chapman
      CD: *Heaven in the Real World*

9. THEME: God's Compassion
   SONG: "I Have Been There"
   ARTIST: Mark Schultz
      CD: *Song Cinema*

10. THEME: God's Faithfulness
    SONG: "Back in His Arms"
    ARTIST: Mark Shultz
       CD: *Song Cinema*

11. THEME: God's Love
    SONG: "Will You Be There?"
    ARTIST: Skillet
       CD: *Alien Youth*

12. THEME: God's Will
    SONG: "Place in This World"
    ARTIST: Michael W. Smith
       CD: *The First Decade: 1983-1993*

Appendices

13. THEME: Independence/Holy Living
    SONG: "America Again"
    ARTIST: Carman
    CD: *The Heart of a Champion*

14. THEME: Materialism/Eternity
    SONG: "Things of This World"
    ARTIST: D.C. Talk
    CD: *Nu Thang*

15. THEME: Missions/Evangelism
    SONG: "Here Am I"
    ARTIST: Mercy Me
    CD: *Almost There*

16. THEME: Perseverance/Spiritual Walk
    SONG: "The Runner"
    ARTIST: Twila Paris
    CD: *Kingdom Seekers*

19. THEME: Salvation/Spiritual Warfare
    SONG: "The Champion"
    ARTIST: Carman
    CD: *The Heart of a Champion*

20. THEME: Salvation/Time's Short
    SONG: "Late Great Planet Earth"
    ARTIST: Plumb
    CD: *Candy Coated Water Drops*

21. THEME: Self-Esteem
    SONG: "Caroline"
    ARTIST: Seventh Day Slumber
    CD: *Once Upon a Shattered Life*

22. THEME: Spiritual Healing/Renewal
    SONG: "Heal Me"
    ARIST: Aaron Jeffrey
       CD: *The Climb*

23. THEME: Spiritual Influence
    SONG: "Hero"
    ARTIST: SuperChick
       CD: *Regeneration*

24. THEME: Standing Up for One's Faith
    SONG: "Pledge Allegiance to the Lamb"
    ARTIST: Ray Boltz
       CD: *Moments for the Heart*

25. THEME: Story of Adam and Eve/the Fall
    SONG: "We Didn't Start the Fire"
    ARTIST: Billy Joel
       CD: *Storm Front*

26. THEME: Suicide
    SONG: "Teenage Suicide"
    ARTIST: DeGarmo & Key
       CD: *D & K*

27. THEME: Volunteer Appreciation
    SONG: "Thank You"
    ARTIST: Ray Boltz
       CD: *Moments for the Heart*

If you find a song with a great message but the words aren't understandable, or if the version is too long, consider asking a choir, ensemble, or soloist to sing it for you live.

Appendix D
Suggestions for Expressing Emotion through Body Language

Emotion	Suggestions for Body and/or Face
Admiration	Head tilts sideways, shoulders might lift as you inhale with closed-mouth smile.
Amazement	Eyes widen, mouth opens or hand covers mouth, might look side to side and then smile.
Anger	Mouth pinches together, eyes squint, nostrils flare, body is rigid, hands may even be clenched into fists.
Anticipation	Bite lip, look around, tap foot, bite nails, sit forward.
Anxiety	Tap foot, bite cheek, play with fingers, look around, don't sit still, eyes blink and look down.
Awe	Mouth open, eyes wide, body frozen.
Boredom	Body slumps loosely, hand to cheek, eyes half-mast, may even yawn.
Compassion	Slight pout, eyes soften, hands may touch person hurting or sit in lap, body points to person hurting.
Curiosity	Body leans forward, bite lip, eyes focused on object.
Defiance	Arms cross, head tilts, body rigid, hip may be tilted to side.
Despair	Body limp, eyes diverted, furrowed brow, face solemn.

Desperation	Eyes sad but open, body leans forward at chest, head cocked up, mouth slightly open, sad.
Disappointment	Mouth pouts, eyes sad and looking down, shoulders slightly slumped.
Disgust	Nostrils flare, mouth pinches into a scowl, eyes narrow, body moves away from object or person.
Embarrassment	Eyes look away, mouth pinches together, body slightly slumps, hands may fidget.
Envy	Body turns slightly from object or person, head turns to look over shoulder, mouth pinches together, eyes narrow.
Fear	Shoulders pull back, head tilts slightly away from object or person, eyes bulge, mouth open as if gasping.
Frustration	See *Anger*.
Greed	Nose and head point up, mouth smiles slightly, eyes narrow, body rigid.
Grief	See *Sadness*.
Guilt	See *Embarrassed*.
Happiness	Mouth smiles, eyes open, head up, back straight.
Hatred	See *Anger*.
Hope	Hands may clasp together, inhale deeply, slight smile, shoulders roll back.
Impatience	Pace, fidget, look at watch, pinch lips.
Indifference	Stare off into space. (See *Boredom*.)
Infatuation	Tilt head to the side, bat eyes, smile.
Jealousy	See *Envy*.

Joy	See *Happiness*.
Loneliness	Posture slumps, mouth relaxes almost in a pout, and eyes look down.
Love	Shoulders back, head slightly tilts sideways, closed-mouth smile, eyes open, may bring hands to chest.
Lust	Eyes bore into object or person, mouth has slight sardonic smile, body leans towards object or person.
Mischief	Eyes look upward to lids, sly smile, head slightly tilts down, shoulder may turn in.
Panic	See *Anxiety* and *Fear*.
Pride	Chest puffs out, head held high, mouth relaxes, nose slightly in the air.
Rage	See *Anger*.
Relief	Long blink of the eyelids while exhaling through the nose and allowing shoulders to sag, might have slight smile.
Shame	Head is down, but eyes may peek up toward object or person, shoulders are slightly slumped.
Shock	Body rigid, mouth and eyes open wide.
Sadness	Mouth frowns, eyes half-mast, shoulders slump, might even cry.

Appendix E
Human Video Resources

The following organizations are well-known for their human videos. Some of them have videos to purchase while others might offer some advice.

Youth With A Mission, San Diego/Baja
100 West 35th Street, Suite C
National City, CA 91950
Phone: 1-888-992-6225
Email: info@ywamsdbaja.org
http://www.ywamsandiegobaja.org

Drama Share
82 St. Lawrence Crescent
Saskatoon, Saskatchewan
S7K 1G5 Canada
Phone: Toll-free 1-877-DO-DRAMA (363-7262)
Email: contactus@dramashare.org
http://www.dramashare.org/products.php?cat_id=264

Master's Commission
Phone: 602-867-9858
http://www.masterscommissionusa.com/human_video.php

Let's Skit Crazy ™
www.ChristianSkitScripts.com/humanvideos.htm

Faith Evangelism Drama Squad (FEDS)
Faith Chapel
9400 Campo Road
Spring Valley, CA 91977
619-461-7451
www.writesftk.com

About the Author

Kimberlee R. Mendoza is an active member of CITA (Christians in Theatre Arts) and the San Diego Christian Writer's Guild. She has been directing drama and human video for almost fifteen years, has written hundreds of scripts for various churches and schools, and has taught playwriting and acting for Christian Youth Theatre.

Her human video script, *The Woman,* was purchased by Youth With A Mission for worldwide distribution. Her plays, *The Mystery of Montley's Manor* and *The Case of the Show-Stopping Nun Nabber,* were published by Contemporary Drama Service, and her scripts, *On the Couch* and *The Coma Companion,* were published in the literary magazine *The Acorn Review.* Her screenplay, *The Seraph War,* was made into a short movie which aired at several venues. Several of her poems have been published in various magazines and anthologies, including "Silent Amour," which won *Creative Arts and Sciences* Editor's Preference Award of Excellence. She is also the author of two novels, *On the Couch* and *The Seraph War.*

Mrs. Mendoza earned a Bachelor of Arts degree in Human Development from San Diego Christian College (formerly Christian Heritage College) and holds a Master's degree in Humanities with an emphasis in Literature and Playwriting from California State University, Dominguez Hills.

Order Form

Meriwether Publishing Ltd.
PO Box 7710
Colorado Springs, CO 80933-7710
Phone: 800-937-5297 Fax: 719-594-9916
Website: www.meriwether.com

Please send me the following books:

_____	**The Human Video Handbook** #BK-B289	$15.95

by Kimberlee R. Mendoza
Christian outreach in dramatic movement and music

_____ **Acting Up in Church** #BK-B282 $15.95
by M.K. Boyle
Humorous sketches for worship services

_____ **Worship Sketches 2 Perform** #BK-B242 $15.95
by Steven James
A collection of scripts for two actors

_____ **More Worship Sketches 2 Perform** #BK-B258 $14.95
by Steven James
A collection of scripts for two actors

_____ **Service with a Smile** #BK-B225 $15.95
by Daniel Wray
52 humorous sketches for Sunday worship

_____ **More Service with a Smile** #BK-B266 $15.95
by Daniel Wray
Another helping of humorous sketches for Sunday worship

_____ **Acts for God** #BK-B274 $15.95
by Howard Shirley
38 dramatic sketches for contemporary services

_____ **On the Edge** #BK-B275 $15.95
by Steven James
A collection of 17 hard-hitting dramatic monologs

These and other fine Meriwether Publishing books are available at your local bookstore or direct from the publisher. Prices subject to change without notice. Check our website or call for current prices.

Name: _____ e-mail: _____

Organization name: _____

Address: _____

City: _____ State: _____

Zip: _____ Phone: _____

❑ **Check enclosed**
❑ **Visa / MasterCard / Discover #** _____

Signature: _____ Expiration date: _____ / _____
(required for credit card orders)

Colorado residents: Please add 3% sales tax.
Shipping: Include $3.95 for the first book and 75¢ for each additional book ordered.

❑ *Please send me a copy of your complete catalog of books and plays.*

Order Form

Meriwether Publishing Ltd.
PO Box 7710
Colorado Springs, CO 80933-7710
Phone: 800-937-5297   Fax: 719-594-9916
Website: www.meriwether.com

Please send me the following books:

_____ **The Human Video Handbook**   #BK-B289 $15.95
by Kimberlee R. Mendoza
Christian outreach in dramatic movement and music

_____ **Acting Up in Church**   #BK-B282 $15.95
by M.K. Boyle
Humorous sketches for worship services

_____ **Worship Sketches 2 Perform**   #BK-B242 $15.95
by Steven James
A collection of scripts for two actors

_____ **More Worship Sketches 2 Perform**   #BK-B258 $14.95
by Steven James
A collection of scripts for two actors

_____ **Service with a Smile**   #BK-B225 $15.95
by Daniel Wray
52 humorous sketches for Sunday worship

_____ **More Service with a Smile**   #BK-B266 $15.95
by Daniel Wray
Another helping of humorous sketches for Sunday worship

_____ **Acts for God**   #BK-B274 $15.95
by Howard Shirley
38 dramatic sketches for contemporary services

_____ **On the Edge**   #BK-B275 $15.95
by Steven James
A collection of 17 hard-hitting dramatic monologs

These and other fine Meriwether Publishing books are available at your local bookstore or direct from the publisher. Prices subject to change without notice. Check our website or call for current prices.

Name: _____   e-mail: _____

Organization name: _____

Address: _____

City: _____   State: _____

Zip: _____   Phone: _____

❏ **Check enclosed**
❏ **Visa / MasterCard / Discover #** _____

Signature: _____   Expiration date: _____ / _____
(required for credit card orders)

Colorado residents: Please add 3% sales tax.
Shipping: Include $3.95 for the first book and 75¢ for each additional book ordered.

❏ *Please send me a copy of your complete catalog of books and plays.*